Ese To MASTER JEFE

From street gang life in SOUTH CENTRAL LOS ANGELES
to U.S. NAVY MASTER CHIEF

RAUL R. RAMOS

ISBN: 978-1-66782-871-8 (print)
ISBN: 978-1-66782-872-5 (eBook)

AUTHOR'S NOTE

I want to be very clear. There is nothing to aspire to in gang life. It is not glamorous. I am not promoting it. But I have to be honest about why I gravitated towards it. I need you to know what was so attractive and alluring that it made me turn against my own flesh and blood. At certain times in my story, you may think I'm trying to make it sound cool, but what you're really hearing is nostalgia and an undying love for my friends and the lost boy I once was. Gang violence is responsible for too many senseless deaths and ruined lives. It takes out the guilty and the innocent indiscriminately. It ruins families and communities and robs young people of their futures.

Part of my motivation to write this is to encourage adults to influence at-risk kids like me. I want you to see the person underneath the tough and angry facade. There is a child in there who has been hurt, disappointed, and made to feel unworthy in more ways than you can count. Intervene early, if possible. Be present in their lives. Guide them towards tasks, activities, and hobbies that feed their self-esteem and foster community building. Give them power and responsibility. They are desperate for some control amidst the chaos in their lives.

But the person I really want to reach with my story looks a lot like me. If you are young and feel invisible and powerless, I'm talking to you. I wrote this for you. I see you. I know your value and potential. You have options you can't see yet. Please don't throw them away on the promises of brotherhood and family from the gangs. The cost is not worth your life and your future. Real brotherhood won't take everything from you, it will give you more than you could ever imagine. Real family builds you into a better person. They challenge you to grow and want to see you accomplish great things. And they don't just wish this for you, they help you access the tools you need, open doors, and create opportunities so you can go further than you think. Hopefully after reading my story you'll believe me.

I also want to be upfront that I have the utmost respect for law enforcement officers doing the right thing. They have an extremely difficult job and some make the ultimate sacrifice while trying to keep our communities safe. But I believe we should hold them to a high standard, and that abuse of power cannot be tolerated. In my story, you'll hear of my experiences running into some "bad apples" on the street. This does not reflect my opinion on the entire profession, it's merely an account of my run-ins with the law. I made mistakes and I accept full responsibility for my actions.

ACKNOWLEDGEMENTS

During the COVID-19 pandemic and the most difficult deployment of my career, I got serious about writing this book. It started with paper and pencil, grew into making notes on my phone, and finally became a word document I slogged away on in the middle of the night. The idea was put into my head over the years by more people that I can count or name. Thank you all for the motivation!

In the early days of my first draft, I reached out to Lorraine Cobcroft, a talented ghostwriter, author, publisher, and more. I'm indebted to her for acting as my mentor and sharing her hard-won wisdom on the book writing game. I'm shocked and honored that she even responded to my inquiry, and everything that came after was a bonus. This book would not have been possible without her.

One of the sailors that crossed my path many years ago in Monterey, California has had the unenviable task of translating my words for the masses. Thank God she's a linguist! Joni Horton encouraged me to write this book when it was just a pipe dream, and offered to help me edit it when that day came. I'm not sure it was a check she ever meant to cash, but I'm grateful that she found my voice and helped me share my story with the world.

I dedicate this book to my two beautiful children, Emily and Raulito. I love you more than life itself. You are the main reason for my drive to succeed. I will give anything so you can have a better life than I did growing up. To my mother, father, sister, and nephews, may God continue to bless you. You're always in my thoughts and prayers. To my best friend and supporter, Lil Man, we're going to ride together 'til the wheels fall off, my boy! To all the homeboys and homegirls from Florence, may God bless you all. Special thanks to the U.S. Navy and all past and present service members for your sacrifices to this great nation. It's been an honor to serve alongside some fine Americans. And last but definitely not least, much love to anyone who has supported the dream that became this book.

GLOSSARY

Chanclas - sandals or flip flops

Tia - Aunt

Tio - Uncle

Throw hands - fist fight

Ese - Mexican slang, often used in inner city Spanish speaking neighborhoods, to address a man, similar to homie, amigo, dude, bro, cholo

Paisas - slang for someone from your country, popular among Mexicans living in the US

Sureños or **South Siders** - Southern California gang members

Tax collecting - a fee or "rent" collected by a gang from all people, gang members or otherwise, selling illicit goods within the gang's territory

Strap - gun

Boys - police officers, cops

Caught slipping - when a rival finds you unprepared or unaware

For Emily, my fighter and Raulito, my mini me with a heart of gold

CONTENTS

CHAPTER 1

In order to understand my story, you must first understand the world I came into. Trauma begets trauma. But I hope, more than anything, by the end of this you believe that the cycle can be broken. I'm living proof.

On April 10, 1952, my mother Alicia was born in Mexicali, Mexico. She lived in a one room, makeshift home with her siblings and her parents, Maria and Luis. My grandfather Luis built their small home out of scrap metal, aluminum, and any wood he managed to find in town. There was no electricity or running water. They boiled water in a huge pot to use for hot showers. All of their laundry was done by hand, and the only "bathroom" they had involved squatting over a hole in the ground behind their home. Luis worked in a local butcher shop and my grandmother Maria cleaned homes for a living. They made just enough money to put food on the table and clothes on their backs.

Luis was an alcoholic and regularly beat the shit out of Maria. So she decided to leave with my mother Alicia and her siblings for southern Mexico. They moved to a small town called El Verde in Sinaloa to live with my mom's grandparents. They had a small farmhouse made of concrete and wood, where her grandfather raised cows, pigs, horses, and chickens. The house had several rooms, but no running water or electricity. There was a river within walking distance where they got their water, did their laundry, bathed, and washed down the farm animals. In recent years, the area has been gentrified by the cartels, but at the time, the roads were just dirt and rocks, and most of the homes were simple, makeshift shacks, one on top of the other. My sister and I actually got to visit once when I was 7 or 8 and it had not changed much since my mother lived there.

Alicia was 3 years old when her mother left her abusive father, but the beatings didn't end there. They got passed on to the next generation. Maria used to beat my mom with anything and everything she could get her hands on including sticks, metal rods, chanclas, and clothing irons. As my mother grew up, their relationship never improved. My mom and her grandmother Sophia never got along well either. By the time my mom was 17, Maria and Sophia conspired together and secretly made a plan to send her away to the United States. They wanted her gone.

Despite this, Alicia was actually excited to start over in America. It represented a new beginning and a chance to finally escape the abuse. But she was also terrified, because she didn't speak English and had no idea what to expect. She was walking blindly into the unknown.

My mother made her way to the U.S. with help from her brother, Gabino, who was already living in Los Angeles, California. He arranged a visa for her, and they flew out of Mazatlan, Mexico. Initially, she stayed with her brother, helping care for his newborn son, Eric. They lived in a nice, middle-class neighborhood with lawns and well-kept homes. Soon after though, my mother found a job through a neighbor and distant family member operating a sewing machine in a local sweatshop. She made 10 dollars a week sewing belts from 6 am to 6 pm, day in and day out. She had no days off. Before too long, the same neighbor helped her find a full-time job in a family-owned Italian restaurant. She assisted with kitchen duties like washing dishes and preparing food. She worked there for several years and was finally able to afford a place of her own in Los Angeles. It may have only been a one bedroom apartment in a rough neighborhood, but it was all her own. Little did she know that my father would be her new neighbor and her life was about to drastically change.

My father, Raul Ramos Sr., was born on June 14, 1957 and was raised in Tamazula, Jalisco, Mexico. Their home had some modern conveniences like electricity, indoor plumbing, hot water, and even a TV. Sadly, his mother died within days of giving birth to him due to unknown health complications after delivery. His father, Ruben, died of throat cancer when my father was only 12 years old. The premature passing of both of his parents would have long term emotional effects on my father. He tried to avoid and numb these feelings with alcohol, but drinking just made it easier for his demons to escape and hurt everyone around him.

After the death of his father, Raul Sr. was raised by various family members including his big sister, Rosa. My Tia Rosa is my favorite auntie of all time. She's always treated me like her own son, but her kindness isn't limited to her family. She has a heart of gold and a hug, smile, or laugh ready for everyone she meets. His Tia Maria and his grandmother Maria-DeJesus also helped raise him after Ruben's death. He had a dog around this age named Sultan that he loved dearly. He would sic his dog on any man that came around looking for his sister Rosa. My father was extremely territorial and protective of his sister, both because she helped raise him and also because they were quite close as they got older.

Raul Sr. never needed a job while growing up in Mexico because his family was middle class and provided my father everything he needed and then some. He even attended a Catholic school for some time, but he never finished. To be honest, he was spoiled and got whatever he wanted. So it's no surprise that by the time he was going into his teenage years, he began to rebel. He could often be found at the local bars, where he was known as a ladies' man, drinking his life away. He was young, naïve, and had a huge ego.

His late father's brother, Tio Leobardo, the head of the family grocery business, told him to go to the United States because he wasn't doing anything positive with his life in Tamazula. Uncle Leobardo enlisted a friend of his to drive Raul Sr. up north to the border near Tijuana, Mexico. From there he was connected with a coyote, someone who helped smuggle immigrants across borders. They took him to a vulnerable spot where he could jump the fence into the U.S. According to my father, he landed in a mud puddle and was completely drenched and covered in muck. He walked to a local gas station and washed up in the bathroom as best he could. Then he began the dreaded walk through the California desert for one full day and night, without food or water. He managed to make it to a northern California city, Mendota, where he called my Tia Rosa to pick him up. She was living in Redwood City, California at the time and had been in the States for several years already. Tia Rosa told me he arrived with burned feet and hole-ridden shoes.

He lived with her and my Tio Miguel for about six months before my father chose to leave of his own accord. He had been butting heads with Tio Miguel because he didn't want to work, so he decided he was ready to move on. He went to Los Angeles where he hooked up with his best friend, Hector. There he found a job with Hector doing interior uphol-stery work on truck campers, but that didn't last long. Shortly after that, he found a job at a gasket manufacturing company in L.A. He started in 1978 and still works there to this day.

One day, my father and his friends were swimming in the pool at their apartment complex. It just so happened that my mother decided to go for a swim that day, too. While all of his friends were openly flirting with her, my father sat back and played it cool, continuing to swim quietly in the pool. After a while, he approached, asked her name, and they talked for some time. He and his friends had planned to make carne asada that night, but didn't have any salt to season it. So he asked my mom if she had some he could borrow. She invited him up to her apartment so he could get the salt, and they started dating soon after. They dated for about two years before they got married. My father was only 18, and my mother was 23. Soon after, they got pregnant with my sister, Lisa.

According to my dad, there were some good times. When I asked my mom, her response was not just no, but hell no. There was never enough money. The relationship became abusive early on. My father continued drinking excessively and partying with his friends. He was also seeing other women. Before she knew it, their marriage started to go down in flames.

CHAPTER 2

My older sister Lisa was born in Los Angeles, California on February 8, 1977. She had dark, thick hair and large brown eyes. She loved being held, especially by my father. She'd cry if you put her down. We were born only a year apart, so naturally we were very competitive. She took my bottles when I was just a baby and got jealous when anyone would hold me. We fought over attention, food, and anything else we saw of value. We were constantly at each other's throats, not just because that's what a lot of young siblings do, but also because we didn't know what a loving relationship looked like.

There were no healthy relationships around us. I'm more than positive that the ass whoopings we witnessed between our parents warped our young minds. We became a product of our environment. From a young age we were full of anger, hate, and hurt, and we took it out on one another. We were the other's easiest target, so we liberally threw verbal abuse and even a few punches at each other from time to time.

I, Raul Ruben Ramos, was born on August 24, 1978. I was named after my father and my middle name came from my late grandfather. I was a very quiet and calm baby. I slept so much that my mother was concerned and asked the doctor if I was okay. But I cried when anyone tried to hold me. I didn't want to be cuddled or touched. I just wanted to sleep in peace.

There was a running joke that I looked like a little girl when I was 3 or 4 years old and that Lisa and I were twin sisters. My hair was really long and thick, just like my father's. That was his style back then. He used to rock bell bottom pants, platform shoes, and long hair with a bandana tied around it. I guess he liked having a mini me, and the hairstyle was part of that.

My mother, father, sister, and I all lived in a small, one bedroom apartment in Los Angeles in a lower-class neighborhood infested with street gangs. By this point, my father was a full-blown alcoholic and drank excessively at every opportunity. He had a family and was working full-time, but still found plenty of opportunities to drink and party with his friends.

I recall a lot of arguing, screaming, and physical abuse between my mother and father on a daily basis. It seemed normal to us. My sister and I would try to get in the middle of it and we were often pushed to the side. I would put my hands over my ears to block out the yelling and close my eyes so I wouldn't see them beat the shit out of each other. It didn't really work, but I had to try. I couldn't tell what they were fighting about, but I can still hear the loud voices and see the slaps they traded.

My father's friends routinely came over to our house to drink with him, and often partied through the night. My sister and I had our first shot of tequila around age 4 or 5 and would often sip on cans of beer that were offered to us by my father and his friends. Or, we would just grab the random cans of beer left laying around our apartment and drink out of those.

Soon the fighting and all the drama between my parents became too much. My father wanted to separate from my mother and often threatened to leave. The situation was unbearable for all of us. My mother was constantly crying. My sister and I were traumatized. My father drank to escape. Finally, one day my father said he was leaving for good. He grabbed his belongings and headed towards his car parked outside. I'll never forget that moment. My sister and I followed him like sad, lost puppies. We were crying the whole way as we tagged along right behind him. My dad started his car and put all of his things in the trunk. He handed his thin, ugly ass, lime green cotton blanket that he slept with to my sister. This was the ugliest blanket I have ever seen. But my sister treasured it and kept it for years. He drove away that night and it was four or five years before we saw him again.

I was 5 years old when he left, and Lisa was 6. I remember the feeling of him leaving as if it were yesterday. But it took years before I could put words to those emotions. I felt sad, hurt, empty, betrayed, upset, abandoned, and confused all at once. It's a lot for anyone to process, much less a 5 year old. I didn't want him to leave. Even with all of the screaming and abuse, he was my father and I wanted him around. I feel like there was so much I missed out on when he left. I remember watching random families. I'd see a father and mother together with their kids and I would feel so angry, knowing my father wasn't around. Knowing they had something I didn't. I lashed out often. I felt like he could have been my protector in so many situations, and maybe shielded my sister and I from some of the struggles we were about to face.

He wasn't around to teach us how to ride a bike or tie our shoes. He didn't teach me how to change the oil in a car or a flat tire, or even how to cook. I missed out on the birds and the bees talk. I wish every boy could talk about it with his father. There is no doubt in my mind that I would have benefitted from some direction in that area of my life. I made so many mistakes and have more regrets than any one person has a right to. Maybe it's wishful thinking that he would have been an involved father if he had stayed. But when he drove away that day, he took any possibility of a close relationship between us with him and he left a hole I tried to fill in all the wrong ways.

I bottled up my feelings about my father leaving for a long time. Probably too long, because when they finally came out, they brought out the worst in me. I held a grudge against both of my parents for years. They were absent during my childhood, when I needed them most. My father because he chose to leave, and my mother because she had to work to support us. To this day, I haven't said I love you to my mother, and vice versa. Neither one of us is emotionally available to the other. My father said I love you to me a few times over the years, but only when he was drinking heavily. Children need to hear and feel those words from their parents, early and often. My sister and I suffered the long term effects of that deficit. We've both paid the price. And instead of rallying around each other after our father walked out, we continued to fight. We were hurt, so we hurt each other.

CHAPTER 3

I was 5 years old and could barely speak English. I learned some words from watching TV at home and from having conversations with people in my neighborhood. My mother enrolled me in the local elementary school about two miles away from our apartment. I absolutely loved going to school. It didn't take me long to learn English, and I was very strong in math. I remember being proud when my teacher praised me for picking it up so fast. The positive feedback felt incredibly good, considering how little of it I was used to getting.

I would walk to school and back, alone more days than not. My mother had asked our neighbor to take me in the morning, and also to pick me up and watch over me until she made it home from work. This lady was like two different people. Around my mother she was friendly and nice, but as soon as mom left, she instantly changed and became mean and nasty. I never told my mom. I don't know why. Maybe I was trying to protect her, and not make her life any harder than it already was. I knew if I told her, she'd be forced to confront the problem, and she'd lose a babysitter she desperately needed. The woman rarely walked me to and from school, but lied to my mom and let her think she did.

One day I was waiting on the playground for the babysitter to come and get me. As usual she didn't, so I left on my own and began to walk to her house. I was about to cross the street when I noticed the light had turned yellow. I thought I needed to hurry up and cross before it turned red. I started to run as fast as I could to beat the light, when a kid from school stuck his foot out to trip me. I flew face first onto the street and slammed into the pavement. As I lay in the street, I could feel that my hands and arms were scraped and bleeding. No one bothered to come and help me and the cars waiting at the light were honking their horns at me as I tried to pick myself up. My nose was leaking like a faucet and blood began to run down my shirt and pants. I walked the two miles to the neighbor's house. Somewhere along the way, I took my shirt off and pinched my nose with it, trying to stop the bleeding as I trudged home.

When I finally knocked on the babysitter's door, she began to yell at me, and it was clear she was more worried about me getting blood in her apartment than she was about me bleeding in the first place. She didn't let me inside, so I sat on her porch while she continued screaming at me. She finally asked me what happened. I told her the story while my head and nose were throbbing and I tried not to think of how much pain I was in. She didn't even bother to help clean me up. When my mother arrived a few hours later, she freaked out when she saw me. I am more than positive my nose was broken. We went home, I showered up, and put ice on my face. The thing I remember most is the burning anger I felt deep down. I felt as if I was completely alone in the world and that no one gave a shit about me. I thought about my father and what he would have done if he was around. And I was all the more angry, because he wasn't.

It wasn't just tough for me at home with my father gone. I noticed my mother was extremely sad and I often caught her crying. I don't know if she was missing my father, or if she was just overwhelmed raising two young children on her own. I believe without even realizing it, she began to distance herself emotionally from my sister and me. Money was really tight. With all the financial stress, she wasn't very maternal or nurturing. She had been working a temporary job when my father left, but got laid off. After that, she bounced from one temporary position to another.

We found ourselves living on government assistance. Welfare consisted of a small check that barely covered the rent, and food stamps that got us some groceries, but not everything two growing kids needed. It wasn't enough to get us through the month. Typical meals in our house were eggs, beans and rice, and tortillas. There was often Kool-Aid with no sugar, butter with no bread, cereal with no milk, and peanut butter with no jelly. But there was no shortage of a thick block of that government cheese. That shit was delicious. I still think about how good it was.

I remember being hungry a lot. But twice a month, when my mother picked up the food stamps, we got our favorite dessert as a treat. It was a package of six square danishes, three on each side. They had white frosting on top, cheese in the center, and the bread was so soft it just melted in our mouths. They were little squares of heaven to us. One day there was one last piece of this coveted sweet bread, and both my sister and I decided that we wanted to eat it without sharing. The argument started in the kitchen. I know I pushed Lisa first. She shoved me in return, I fell into the living room, and then the hands started throwing away. It wasn't uncommon for us to fight, but we were both ready to bleed for that last danish.

Sometimes when I got hungry and there was no food at home, I would head to the local liquor store at the corner. I used to stroll in like I was just browsing, put a Twinkie in my pocket, and walk to the back of the store. I'd stuff my face with it, then walk out like nothing had interested me. Those Twinkies were bomb! When I think about it now, I'm pretty sure the owner was watching me and would simply let it go. He caught me once and didn't give me a hard time about it. He just told me not to do it again.

As tough as the day to day was, it should come as no surprise that holidays didn't exist in our home. Thanksgiving, Christmas, and birthdays were never a thing. There were no Christmas trees or presents in our apartment. We simply couldn't afford it. Forget about a Thanksgiving meal, we couldn't even buy the turkey. A holiday was just like any other day to me. I still cringe when people sing the "Happy Birthday" song at parties.

And since money was tight, my moms would buy school clothes for my sister and I from the local Goodwill, a thrift shop. Now this was before thrift shops and vintage clothes got cool. Then it was just hand-me-down clothes and household items for cheap. The clothes she bought from there never fit us very well. My pants were usually "high waters." They were so short it looked like I was prepared for the coming flood. The other kids at school always made fun of my clothes and shoes. I used to rock those no-name-brand, Payless shoe store shoes, while other kids got new and trendy footwear. Let me tell you man, kids are brutal. They used to clown the hell out of me. And every time it happened, I could feel the well of anger, deep down inside, burn and grow. I couldn't control what was happening at home since my father left. And on top of it, I had to pay the price at school because I couldn't afford to have cool stuff.

Back to school day was the worst. All the kids were excited to show off their new school gear: backpacks, outfits, shoes, folders, and lunch boxes. I never had any of that, and I remember feeling embarrassed in my same old clothes. We didn't go back to school shopping. There was no money for new anything.

Every Friday we had a show-and-tell in our class. Most of the boys would bring the hottest new toys like GI Joe figurines and Transformers. They were all toys I wished I had, but my mom wasn't able to buy them. But one day, I finally decided I was going to participate in show-and-tell. I remember I was so excited. At Goodwill, they had plastic bags filled with random toys that my moms would sometimes get for me. So before my big show-and-tell debut, I grabbed several toys from the bag, took them apart, and put them together as one. I presented my creation as if it were a new Transformer. One of the kids called me out and said it was NOT a Transformer, then all the others piled on and made fun of me. I felt so ashamed.

When I got home, I told my mom what happened and I could see the hurt in her face. I know she wished she could buy the toys my sister and I wanted. I never doubted she really wanted to provide for us. One day soon after, we all went to a department store in the local mall. Lisa found a Barbie doll she desperately wanted, and carried it all through the store. I was clutching a Voltron, a super robot made out of five lion robots that interlocked as one. This was one of my favorite cartoons that I watched on Saturday mornings. My mother told my sister and me to put both toys in a bag. Then we walked out of the department store without paying for them. The moment we stepped out the alarms went off. We picked up our step and didn't look back until we were several hundred feet away in an adjacent parking lot. Fortunately, security didn't come for us. Why, I have no idea.

I remember my heart pounding out of my chest. I think I was probably 7 years old. I couldn't believe what had happened. No one spoke. We got in my mom's car and went home. This is not easy to say, and it's harder to remember. I know it was wrong, but it showed me that my mom wanted, more than anything, to give us everything our little hearts desired. This does not justify our actions. What we did was wrong, but my adult heart shatters for my mom when I think of it. Her desperation to make us happy in the midst of her own struggle is clear to me. And now that I'm older, I wish I had appreciated what I did have instead of worrying about what I didn't. I wish I hadn't paid so much attention to the other kids.

But I also need to cut that little guy some slack. I was just a kid, struggling with a less-than-ideal home life and growing more aware of our poverty. Gratitude wasn't a lesson that was ever taught to me, but it's one I've tried hard to instill in my own kids and anyone I mentor. Find gratitude for what you do have and focus on building up others in your community. I'm truly grateful for the sacrifices my mother made to provide for us. I know she did the best she could with what she had.

My mother eventually lost her job again. We moved a few miles away and my sister and I enrolled in a new school. My mom was dating again at this point and even started seeing an ese named Jamie from a local gang. He was actually pretty cool and would sometimes steal food from the local grocery store when we were hungry and didn't have anything in the fridge. I saw it with my own eyes one day. He stuffed about four packs of beef in the front of his pants and under his shirt and walked right out of the grocery store. He made dinner for us with it that night.

Around this time, I was in first grade and would often be sent home for not showering, having dirty fingernails and clothes, and sometimes for putting too much vaseline in my hair. We couldn't afford gel, so I used vaseline instead. No one taught me to do this, I just figured out on my own that it worked kind of like hair gel. One day it was blazing hot out and the vaseline basically melted and started to drip down my head, so the school sent me home.

My mother was totally disengaged from her maternal responsibilities, so my sister and I just figured life out on our own. We didn't do a very good job of it. I hardly ever took a shower or ate breakfast. There were so many days my stomach would growl all through class because I was hungry and hadn't eaten. Tortillas were my life saver. There was almost always a pack of them in the fridge. I would throw a few at a time on the stove, warm them up, blacken them just slightly, and then spread on some butter. That was the business! If we were lucky enough to have milk, then milk and tortillas always hit the spot.

Going home from school was never a pleasure. It was horrible. I'll never forget turning on the lights in our apartment and watching cockroaches scramble for cover. The worst was when we went to grab cereal and roaches would come running out of the cereal box. Most of the time it didn't even matter that the cereal was ruined, because we didn't have milk for it anyways.

Despite all of this, I had fun in first grade. I was one of the fastest runners in school and could solve multiplication problems in class quicker than anyone else. I loved field trips, but one in particular always stuck with me. All of the other kids' parents sent paper bags filled with their lunch. I didn't have a sack lunch that day, or on any other field trip for that matter. The teacher's aide noticed and gave me the apple from her own lunch. She felt terrible that I didn't have anything to eat. She may have been the only one to ever notice. I wish I could track her down and thank her. I've never forgotten her or her kindness.

CHAPTER 4

I found myself on the streets outside our apartment a lot after school. With my father gone and Mom always working, I did as I pleased. I usually played with the local neighborhood kids, who were rowdy, rough around the edges, and always talking shit. To me, they seemed like a bunch of rotten, mean ass kids looking to create havoc in the neighborhood. But most of them were probably struggling with the same things I was.

One day I was playing outside with my neighbor and a boy who lived across the street from us. We got bored and decided to hang out in the parking garage in my apartment complex. They both started to deflate the tires on a car in one of the parking spots. A man who lived in the complex approached us and asked us what the hell we were doing, so we all took off running in different directions. I ran further down the street to an empty lot and just hung out for a bit until the dust settled.

It was getting dark, so I started to walk home. My mom let me in, and within an hour, an angry mob of neighbors had gathered outside our door, yelling for my mom to come out. They banged on our door and the living room window. I was so scared I locked myself in the bathroom. But I could still hear the pounding and shouting from there. My mom opened the bathroom door and asked me if I had flattened all the tires on the street. Apparently more than 30 cars had flat tires and the man who saw us blamed me instead of the boys that had actually deflated the tires in the garage. The residents wanted my mom's head on a stick and continued to pound on all of our windows and damn near kicked our door down.

After a while, the police showed up and deescalated the situation. They talked to my mother and she insisted that I would never do anything like that and that I didn't have the means to do so. I remember the comfort I felt, knowing that she had my back. The police officers filed a report and moved on. But from then on, everyone in the neighborhood looked at and treated us differently. None of the neighborhood kids wanted to hang out or play with me anymore. I'm guessing their parents told them to stay away.

Without any neighborhood friends, I started getting involved with another crowd right outside our apartment complex. There was a long brick wall that the neighborhood eses would hang out on. Some would be squatting down in their ese pose in front of the wall. Others stood up in their ese stance, while a few would sit along it. There was usually a beer wrapped in a paper bag in someone's hand and music bumping loud from a nearby parked car. They were all dressed gangstered down from head to toe. The gang attire consisted of oversized, heavily starched and creased khaki pants, Stacy Adams shoes, a Pendletons shirt with only the top button closed, and a white shirt underneath. They used hair nets to help keep their hair slicked back, and kept a dark-colored bandana, nicely folded and creased, hanging out of their front and back pockets. Almost all of them had tattoos on their hands and arms. I couldn't help but notice the beautiful women hanging out with them and the well-kept cars parked close by. Ever since, I've always had an eye for nice cars and dreamed of driving one myself. Cars became a life-long obsession.

One of the eses sitting on the wall noticed me and called me over to him. He asked me to take a drink of his Budweiser. It was really cold and tasted delicious. I tried to down it all at once and his homeboys started laughing. They had no idea I was already an experienced drinker by age five. They seemed as if they got along well. From where I was sitting, it looked like a calm, peaceful, and tight-knit familia. They looked out for one another and had each other's back. Everything I was missing. This was my first introduction to gang life.

It fascinated me. Every time I stepped out of my apartment, I made a point to go and sit with them. They started to send me to the liquor store to buy munchies for them. I loved it. The best part was that I would buy snacks for myself too, and after I delivered theirs, I almost always got to keep the change. Occasionally they gave me their pocket change too, just because. The eses were always cool to me and it was nice to have a warm welcome somewhere. To feel seen and appreciated. If they had food and snacks, they never hesitated to offer me some. I felt like I belonged. It felt like family. A family I wanted to officially be part of one day.

Over the next few years in elementary school, street gangs started to become more and more active around the school and in my neighborhood.

I was steered away from the gangs for a time however, thanks to some new friends across the street named Larry and Eddie. The brothers were hardcore into skateboarding and really pushed me to get into it. Larry was probably 16, tall and slim, with black hair and bad acne. He was kind, calm, and always happy. Eddie was the younger brother at about 13. He had braces, darker skin than Larry, and thin black hair. Though he was sensitive, he was also very goofy and fun. When he was trying to master a new trick on the skateboard, he could get sullen when it wasn't going well. The boys accepted me and took me under their wing. I looked up to them as if they were my big brothers.

With their help, I picked up skateboarding quickly. Larry and Eddie even gave me one of their really cool skateboards when I told them my moms couldn't afford to buy me one. It was a Powell-Peralta, which is still a very popular skateboard. There were days where we would just skateboard for miles and miles with no direction or plan. We were free and would just go. We were always trying to find the steepest hills to skate down and the biggest ramps to ride and jump off. We'd go to local schools and ride all over the yards. The skateboard movie *Thrashin'* from 1986 really inspired us and we'd often try to emulate it.

Larry and Eddie's mom was a very small Filipina woman, no taller than 5 feet. She always walked around looking like she wanted to spank me. I must have charmed her eventually, because she finally opened up and was really sweet to me. Their dad was older, a tall white man with white hair. He was retired military and had a garage full of GI Joe figurines he'd collected.

Sadly, the fun with these two didn't last too long. Eddie and Larry moved away to a city that was about a three-hour skateboard ride away. I skated there several times, but no one ever answered the door. The first time was a bit scary because I'd never been that far away from home on my own. Larry got a girlfriend and Eddie lost interest in skateboarding. They grew apart from me and life moved on. So I gave up the skateboard life and turned my attention back to the eses on the street.

I started to dress like an ese in fourth grade. Maybe if I walked like one, dressed like one, acted like one, and talked like one, I would be welcomed into the family. The gangs could give me what I was missing. They were friends, fathers, mentors, and a way to figure out how to be a man all wrapped up in one package. I was officially a wannabe ese. I admired all of the gang graffiti around my neighborhood. When I was in class, I'd turn my paper over and doodle graffiti constantly, while I daydreamed about being a gang banger. I'd practice writing my last name in Old English style letters, block capitals, and calligraphy.

We moved yet again. It was around this time my father started showing up. He said he wanted to be a part of our lives. The fact that the court system caught up to him and forced him to pay child support probably had something to do with it, too. The money he provided wasn't much, but it went towards the rent check. Initially, I wanted no part of the dude. But it was cool to see him again. He invited me to his house in Huntington Park, a neighboring community of South Central Los Angeles. He was living with a couple of paisas in a place right off Florence Avenue. This street and the gang named for it would soon change my life forever.

After my initial hesitation, I ended up staying a whole weekend with him. When we woke up in the morning, my father taught me how to make huevos rancheros. The ingredients were simple but delicious. He sautéed fresh onions, tomatoes, and chili serrano with a bit of fresh garlic. Then he threw in a half dozen eggs and scrambled away. He had corn tortillas ready to go and we tore into it. It was the best meal I'd had for as long as I could remember. For years after, I made my eggs the same way. This one breakfast with my father stuck with me that much.

Then my dad and his paisa friends started drinking. I could see things hadn't really changed after all. So, I decided to go for a stroll. I walked a few blocks up the way on Florence Avenue. This portion of it in Huntington Park was really dark and dirty. It was covered in graffiti and there were stray dogs running loose. Most of the shops were small businesses, usually owned by immigrants trying to make a go of it. On just about every corner you could find a liquor store, taco stand, prostitutes, and crack heads.

I headed west to the corner of Florence and Pacific Boulevard. I've never seen anything like it. Pacific Boulevard was a long street filled with outdoor and indoor department stores. It was like an outdoor mall. There were a bunch of eses out there, heavily tatted up and selling social security cards, drivers licenses, green cards, and drugs. You name it, they had it. One of the eses had a jersey on with embroidery that said Florencia 13 Gangsters and I noticed the graffiti all around me said the same thing.

The crowds of people and shoppers were so deep that you rubbed shoulders with damn near everyone out there. I later found out that Pacific Boulevard was my father's jam. He hung out there, specifically at the hole-in-the-wall bars. My father was a pool shark with surprisingly well-honed skills and he used to hustle paisas for money. He would pretend to be an average player to a stranger, make a bet with them, and walk away with their lunch money. More often than not, this ended with him throwing hands. But my father was a big man and had some heavy hands on him. He was a bar brawler and was feared because of it. That was another one of his hustles. He'd challenge a stranger to a fight for money and almost always won easily. He would get completely wasted in these bars and spend every penny he had living in the fast lane. I've pulled him out of those same bars more times than I can count. I'd drag him home and lay him down so he could recover from his bender.

I loved that weekend with my father. I had spent so many years wishing he was a part of my life. Now he was coming around again and it felt like a new beginning. It was, but I had no idea the turn my life was about to take.

CHAPTER 5

People that are familiar with Hispanic street gangs but haven't lived the life usually think they only operate on the East Side of Los Angeles. This could be due to movies like *American Me, Colors, Blood In Blood Out*, and *Boulevard Nights*. It's not as well known that South Central Los Angeles is dominated by Hispanic gangs due to a large Hispanic population there. South Central LA has long been known for its African American gangs, through movies like *Boyz n the Hood* and *Menace II Society*, and also because of heavy media coverage of the gang war between the Bloods and the Crips. But they aren't the only street gangs vying for control of this part of LA.

Some time in the 1940's, a large number of Hispanic immigrant workers were hired by the railroad companies to lay down tracks throughout Los Angeles county. They settled from Los Angeles all the way to Long Beach. A large portion ended up living in South Central, and the Hispanic community eventually outnumbered the African American population.

South Central La Florencia 13 gang or the F13 gang is a hardcore street gang that was established in the Florence-Firestone area of South Central LA and consists of various cliques. Cliques are groups within the gang, or sub groups, that are spread out on multiple streets throughout the Florencia territory. Florencia has many cliques, each with their own name like the Malditos, Termites, Bagos, Locos, Gangsters, Jokers, Tokers, Midnights, 64th Street, and many more. Each clique is made up of anywhere from a dozen to hundreds of members.

The F13 gang is so big that most of the members don't know each other personally and sometimes even rival against each other from within. There's always been competition over whose clique is bigger and badder. Most conflicts from within Florencia would start up at Florence parties when everyone was lit and hyped up. More often than not, conflicts were settled by throwing hands, and then squashed. I was involved in one or two of these street boxing battles back in my day with homeboys from other cliques. F13 has more than 3,000 documented members. Their rivals are several large gangs that spread throughout all of LA county, some located within blocks and across the train tracks from F13 territory. F13 got its name from Florence Avenue, a major street that runs east and west through several cities in Los Angeles county. The name also comes from the fact that it started in the Florence-Firestone section of LA. The theme song for F13 gang members is "Florence" from an old school music group, The Paragons. It's played regularly at parties to announce F13 presence and on the radio as both tribute and as a challenge to any rivals listening.

The Florencia gang name is followed by the number "13" to show strong allegiance to a prison gang of a higher echelon. The 13th letter of the alphabet is "M", which clearly indicates the connection to the prison gang. Many of the early members of that gang were recruited from the Florencia gang, and still are. All hardcore Southern California gangs that pay allegiance to the prison gang are called Sureños, and represent that connection by using the number 13. F13 has expanded outside of South Central and into various states in the U.S. and even into Mexico. The Florencia 13 gang is easily among the top three largest street gangs, along with gangs like MS13 and 18th Street.

The money that supports the gang comes from many avenues including, but not limited to, drug slanging, tax collecting, armed robberies, selling green cards or social security cards, and home invasions. In 2007, the F13 gang was investigated in an undercover sting called Operation Joker's Wild. This was the largest street gang bust in American history that involved over 100 F13 gang members being taken into custody. By this time, I had already been in the Navy for 9 years. I remember hearing about it from my best friend and seeing the news online. I always wondered what would have happened to me if I were still caught up in the streets of Florence.

A shit load of F13 members were convicted under the federal Racketeer Influenced and Corrupt Organizations, or RICO act. Their trials focused on F13 street gang business that included drug trafficking, attempted murder, murder, and extortion. It also covered F13's criminal enterprise and its control by imprisoned higher echelon members and those on the street. Leaders of F13 collected taxes or "rent" from its own members and anyone who dared to sell in F13 territory. There were numerous law enforcement agencies involved in Operation Joker's Wild such as the FBI, DEA, U.S. Marshals, ICE, the Los Angeles police department, IRS-Criminal Investigations Division, the Bureau of Alcohol, Tobacco, Firearms and Explosives, and several more. This operation put a huge dent in the F13 territory and took a chunk of its members off the street. But like any organization, when key players are taken down, there's always someone in line behind them ready to step up, take the helm, and continue to take care of business.

CHAPTER 6

I was introduced to Downer and Gato from F13 MDS, the Florencia 13 Malditos clique, by some mutual friends. Downer and Gato, which means "cat" in Spanish, were two hardcore white boys. I was initially confused because F13 was a predominantly Hispanic gang. I had no idea they let white boys in. But these two eses were different. They might have been white on the outside, but they were definitely brown on the inside. They were without a doubt the downest white eses I've ever met. They had no fear and proved it on the daily, without hesitation.

I started to hang out with them more and more, and soon began to follow in their footsteps. Before I knew it, I took a drive to South Central with them, specifically to 58th Street. This is where the original Malditos clique was born. Malditos has many meanings depending on how you use it in a sentence. It can mean cruel, mean, evil, cursed, damned, or bad when translated into English. To be part of this clique in F13, you were initiated or "jumped in," meaning you had to take a beating for a certain number of seconds and hold your own. You also needed to go on a mission or put in work on your rivals. To put in work meant that you were doing something that was hurting an enemy or rival, which in turn gave you bragging rights in the gang or earned you respect from your homeboys. Once you were in, you were in for life. You couldn't just walk away. The only out was under special circumstances such as family ties. Sometimes heavy hitting VIPs had younger family members that joined the gang. If that younger person then wanted out, the VIP could vouch for them and they'd get a free hall pass. You had to be ruthless, cold-blooded, and ready to die for the gang and everything it stood for. You could never show weakness to the homeboys, rivals, or anyone else.

I'll never forget pulling up to 58th Street that night. It was surreal. It was exactly like I imagined it would be. The homeboys were everywhere on the block, at least 40 to 50 heads deep. They were in the middle of the street, all over the sidewalks, and standing up against a fence. The street lights were shot out, graffiti was everywhere, the alleyways completely trashed, and the sound of loud music came banging out of the trunks of several nearby cars. It appeared as if everyone was having a good time. I could see that some of the homies were slanging weed and they had a lot of buyer traffic coming through. Customers came on foot or drove through to pick it up. It was like there was no law in sight, like you'd expect from a third world country. They owned this block.

I remember the feeling of being nervous, adrenaline rushing, but I also felt like I belonged. There were girls from out of town there to visit, hanging around with the eses. I could see the bullet holes in the wall where the graffiti block letters tagged this as F13 territory. They reached about 20 feet high and spanned around 50 feet long. There was no grass in sight, and so many stray dogs that they were running around in packs. I've never seen anything like it, only imagined it. I remember looking up at the power lines and thinking I saw a cat up there. After taking a closer look, I realized it was actually a huge rat. The ghetto bird, what we called the police helicopter, was circling in the air as it often was in this neighborhood. Actually, multiple ghetto birds were in the air surveilling that night, and I'd bet money they were chasing someone down. The homies were drinking 40's and smoking weed. A few were even smoking "water", the street name for PCP.

I was dressed down for the occasion - sporting black and white Nike Cortez on my feet, and size 38 inch waist, crisply creased Ben Davis pants. My actual waist size was closer to 28 inches then. I was rocking a large, black Ben Davis shirt, and wearing some black "murder gloves." We called them that because every time we put in work on our rivals, we wore them. They were actually just cheap, black cotton garden gloves and we all thought they went hard with our Ben Davis suits. And of course I was rocking the shaved head.

I was introduced to most of the homies on the block. Some welcomed me, while others not so much. Some asked me how old I was because I looked so young. I was ten years old going on 11. Someone handed me a 40 ounce Budweiser, my first 40 of beer ever, and I felt obligated to drink it all. Honestly, it was kind of warm so it tasted like shit. But I drank it anyway. I remember feeling more buzzed than a motherfucker. Holy shit man. The night passed and before I knew it, it was about 4 am.

I met the homeboy Yogie through Downer that night. I thought he was cool. I remember clearly that he was rocking a Los Angeles Raiders hat, because I wanted to buy the exact same one. He offered Downer, Gato, and me a place to stay for the night and we gladly accepted. I woke up with a mean ass headache, thirsty, and hungry as fuck. The homeboys Yogie and Downer were already awake. Yogie cooked up some eggs and had some kool-aid with no sugar. Man, that was the best breakfast I had since my father cooked for me! I was truly grateful for Yogie's hospitality.

This became our weekend ritual, hanging out in the hood. And hopefully soon, I would be welcomed officially into the "family." Unfortunately for Gato he was busted and did some time. I have never seen or heard from him since. There was a rumor that he started using drugs, got messed up in the head, slaughtered his whole family, and ended up in a mental institution. Downer stayed out of jail for a time, but not for long. He ended up doing time, but not before he helped make me an official member of the F13 Malditos.

CHAPTER 7

It was a Friday evening and I was chilling at my mom's house, waiting to leave for the South Central hood. I was ready to get my 58th Street hit for the week. I had some Brenton Wood oldies playing in the background while I creased the shit out of my Ben Davis pants and shirt with a hot, steaming iron. My iron always had plenty of water, because the steam, along with a bottle of starch, gave me super sharp creases. I wiped down my Nike Cortez shoes, specifically the soles, so they were a bright white. No way would I allow for my Nikes to be dingy. I made sure my buzz cut was crisp, clean, and freshly trimmed.

I was ready to go, anxiously pacing around waiting for my homeboy to arrive. Downer came through and swooped me up. He'd gotten a ride from a friend of his. There was a house party going down that night in the hood. House parties were the norm, especially on the weekends, but this party and this weekend were special. It was Friday the 13th, making it "F13 day." Many special things go down on F13 day, including parties and making surprise visits to rivals. The Paragon's song "Florence" was always played at Florence parties, but especially on F13 day.

These parties were normally held in a long driveway and sometimes in abandoned lots and warehouses, because most homies didn't have huge backyards. The Malditos especially would always roll deep to parties. We were rowdy, loud and proud, and always announced our arrival by screaming out "Mallldddddiiitttooossss" to let everyone know we were in the house. Malditos were known by all cliques for throwing hands in Florencia. We had some heavy hitters and could punch fools out like no other. Some of the best street fighters I've ever seen are some of the homies from the Malditos and Florencia overall. Maybe I'm biased, but I think a lot of them could have had careers in fighting, like MMA or professional boxing, no bullshit. Lil Man, my best friend, was one of them. He's living proof that size doesn't matter in a street fight. He lived by the saying "the bigger they are, the harder they fall." He used to knock fools out twice his size. Malditos that I remember who could throw hands were Scooby, Rocky Rene, Poison,

Smokes, Crow, Tricky, Boxer, Big Cyco, Lil Cyco R.I.P., and Koopa R.I.P., to name a few.

That particular night the party was going down at the homie Pokey's house. There was a long driveway that led to his backyard and garage. Aside from that, there was an open concrete floor that we used as the dance floor, and behind the garage there was a dirt lot with weeds and trash everywhere. The homeboys Fat Boy R.I.P. and Big Wicked were on DJ duty that night, bumping some old school music. It was a bit early for the party to start when we arrived, so not many people were there yet. As it got later, the party started to get full of the homies. Little by little more showed up from different cliques, like the 64th Street Locos, Midnight Street Boys, Malos, and some homeboys from the Bagos. As usual, there were out of town girls who dropped in and immediately hit the dance floor with the homies. In the air, you could smell the water and weed being smoked, and just about everybody was walking around with a 40 wrapped in a paper bag. The party had started to die down a bit when my homeboy Downer approached me and asked me if I was ready to be jumped into the hood. I responded that fuck yes, I was more than ready, let's go!

Being jumped into the hood would mean I was officially part of the gang. There was no turning back, and there were serious consequences if I wanted out at any point. I was stating that I would be willing to give up my life for this gang if necessary. I was taking an oath to take care of business if ordered to do so, whether I liked it or not. It was understood that I would show no weakness or fear in any situation, and bring no discredit upon the hood whatsoever. This meant I would challenge anyone I didn't know. I'd ask them what gang they were from if they appeared to be a gang member. If they responded by announcing a rival, it was on and cracking right on the spot. Anywhere, anytime, rain or shine it was on. I was also taking an oath to be loyal to the gang and put in work on our rivals. I was expected to be present at any F13 meetings that were announced, or take the consequences of a beating. It also meant that I would contribute any profit I made in the hood towards straps, which is what we called guns, and taxes. These could be due at any given time.

It was time to get jumped in. Downer let the homeboys know I was ready. Three Malditos would be selected to put a serious beat down on me for 45 seconds. 30 seconds to become a member of Florencia 13, and 15 seconds to become a member of the Malditos clique. I had no choice but to take it like a grown man. Keep in mind I was only 11 years old and probably weighed 140 pounds soaking wet. The homie Largo, which means long in Spanish, who stood about 6 feet 2 inches tall, and the homies Big Wicked and Lil Sleepy were called to the backyard. We gathered in the lot where all the dirt, weeds, and trash had collected.

This beating was the longest 45 seconds of my entire life. I don't recall who, but one of the homies volunteered to count out loud and boy did that man take his time counting. All four of us took off our shirts and were left in tank tops a.ka. "wife beaters." I stood in the middle of all three of them. Lil Sleepy was directly in front of me, toe to toe, while Largo stood behind me, with Big Wicked to my side. We all put our fists up, ready to go. I remember the anxiety and fear pounding through my heart, but I knew I couldn't show it.

The homie in charge of counting said "go" and all I remember is Lil Sleepy connected with a punch right between my eyes that dazed the fuck out of me. My nose immediately started leaking. I managed to remain standing on my own two feet for several more seconds. My head was spinning and in excruciating pain from the punch between my eyes and from the blows and kicks I was still receiving to my upper body. Around the 20 second mark, my homie Largo grabbed me from behind, right around my legs just below my knees, and he lifted me up and slammed me down on my back. My head pounded into the ground. The homie was counting 25, 26, 27, 28, 29, when homeboy Wicked grabbed me and picked me up off the ground as I swung out with punches as best I could. I somehow grabbed a hold of Wicked so I wouldn't fall to the ground again and received yet another pounding on every exposed part of my body from Largo and Lil Sleepy. I managed to get some licks in, but nothing near what I got in return.

And then, it was all over. 45 seconds were up. I had thought they would never end. I was left with a busted nose and eye, and what felt like a concussion. My body was black and blue from head to toe, and I had a badly bruised ego. I stood back up on my two feet and got hand shakes all around, as my homies congratulated me for joining the hood. They gave me the nickname "Chico," which means boy, small, or little, depending on how you use it. I really was a little ese compared to most of the homies. I wasn't even a teenager yet.

I didn't know it was possible to feel so much pride at the same time as being completely nauseated, with my head and nose bleeding and throbbing. I was sporting ripped, dirty pants, my wife beater was completely torn off, and some dirty ass Nike Cortez shoes. But I was officially an active gang member. Gang banging was my occupation, and from that point on I seized every opportunity to bang at any cost, any day, anywhere, rain or shine.

Everyone slowly started to clear out of the party. Before I knew it, it was just Downer and me, wondering how we were going to get home. Home was about a 30 minute drive away. The ride that brought us to the party took off early. Downer and I parted ways that night and I ended up hopping on the metro rail on Florence Avenue to get back to my mother's house. I didn't know it then, but just a few months later, Downer would be in jail for a serious crime.

I'll never forget the looks I got on that train ride home. They covered the full spectrum, from some people feeling bad for me and wanting to help, to confusion, fear, and all the way to disgust. Even with taking the train, I still had to walk about another hour to get home. I remember I knocked on the door and my moms answered. She took one look at me and started to cuss me out in Spanish. But the look of concern on her face told me she wasn't only angry. I just laid down in the middle of the living room floor. I was exhausted and in extreme pain. When I finally fell asleep on the floor, I crashed out for almost 24 hours.

Mom had an idea it was coming. She had tried to intervene so many times, but everything she said went in one ear and out the other. I was too young for my driver's license, but I still took her car to drive to the hood. She physically tried to restrain me many times, but I just shrugged her off and kept it moving. I was single-minded and neither she nor anyone else could have stopped me.

Young kids join street gangs for several reasons. Most join because they're lacking something in their life. A father figure, attention, mentorship, or guidance. Peer pressure and bad influences can play a role as well. I joined a gang because I wanted a sense of belonging. I wanted to be cool and part of something that was bigger than me, instead of feeling left out.

I wanted to feel like I was part of a family, because I'd never really had one. I felt like I had mentors and big brothers for the first time. I had little brothers and sisters too that could look up to me and count on me. It was everything I'd been looking for.

I loved the attention I got everywhere I went. I'd felt invisible, and now everyone could see me. I didn't care if it was negative attention. I had always been fascinated with the lifestyle, since I'd first met those eses out in front of our apartment. I would be able to make easy money, and put some distance between me and the boy who had to make his own Transformers. I would have forceful backup if shit went down and I needed it. Instead of the lonely kid with an absent father and a mother who worked too much. I wanted to rebel and be a bad boy. Not the hurt boy. I longed for the power the gang could give me. Little did I know the next nine years of my life would be a hell of a roller coaster ride on the streets of South Central, where only the strong survive, and even the strong die.

CHAPTER 8

I was supposed to start 7th grade on that Monday, a week after getting jumped into F13. This would end up being the last grade in public school I would attend. I showed up to school with my face still all fucked up from my beat down. There was a beloved security guard named Melinda at the school who always looked out for me. She had a great rapport with all the students, especially gang members, because she kept it real and talked to us with dignity and respect. She treated everyone on campus with equal care and concern. And man let me tell you, she was one tough cookie. She broke up countless fights among some big boys with no problem.

She knew what the deal was when she saw my face, because I had told her I wanted to get jumped into Florencia 13. I had a great relationship with her and trusted her like no other. Her face said it all that morning. She was disappointed in me, but had known it was just a matter of time. She was sad it had finally happened, and I knew she was worried about where I would end up and what would become of me.

School was never my forte. I can't remember anything academically between 4th and 7th grade. I was kicked out of two schools, mostly because of my gang ties. The first time I was kicked out of school, I got caught with a long, sharpened screwdriver. There was some fool from a rival gang that I had beef with. I had that screwdriver in my sock and I was going to shank, or stab, him with it once the after-school bell rang. I was bragging about it in class and before I knew it, security came into class, roughed me up, and took the shank right out of my sock. It was about 15 inches long, stuffed in my shoe and sock. When I went to the principal's office, I was notified that I wouldn't be allowed to return to school. That was the last time I would see Melinda in a school setting.

I'm grateful we kept in touch, though. Melinda didn't drop me just because I was kicked out of school. She invited me to her home and introduced me to her family. Many adults turned away from me once I started gang banging, but it just made me appreciate the ones that stayed interested in my life even more. I can't thank them enough for continuing to care about me even after I became pretty unloveable.

I was given an opportunity to attend 7th grade at another school, but was kicked out again within a short time. I thought I was a badass. I was often chased by rival gangs after school and was involved in several fights during the school day. One day, I was told by another student that there was a fool in a different class disrespecting F13. He was from a gang in Watts, one of Florencia's many rivals. I literally got up from my seat during the middle of class, walked over to woodshop where he was, looked him in the eye and told him that when the bell rang, we were going to get down like James Brown. He needed to get his dancing shoes on.

Once the bell rang, I ran out of my classroom and proceeded to the open ground. The rumor had spread like wildfire that there was going to be a fight so there was already a huge crowd there. He showed up not too long after. We both took our shirts off and went toe-to-toe, exchanging punch for punch. The dude reached down, grabbed my legs, and slammed me on the ground in such a way that we fell together. When we landed, his gun came flying out of his pants. By this time, I could see security coming towards us in the distance. We both got up, he ran towards his gun and I started running towards the exit gate. I hopped the fence and never looked back. They called my mother later that day and told me never to come back to school. This was the last regular school I ever went to.

For a while after, I tried to enroll in several different schools, but was rejected every time. No one wanted to take a chance on me with my record. After that, I was like fuck school and everybody in it. I was frustrated. But something deep down inside told me to stick it out and finish school, because it would pay dividends later on down the road. I listened to my inner voice, which sounded suspiciously like my mom, and sure enough an opportunity came later in my life. I have to give credit to my mother. Even though I never wanted to listen to her, and everything she said fell on deaf ears, she always pushed me to stay in school. I don't remember how I even found the program, but the Los Angeles County School District had an alternative school program during this time for kids with similar situations.

I'll never forget the teacher who ran the program. Her name was Miss "G." She motivated me to do well, because she didn't let me get away with shit. She could tell if I half-assed my work and demanded I do better. But she also praised me when I did, and it made me want to make her happy. She let me know she had faith in me. She believed I could make something of my life and constantly reminded me that I needed my diploma to do it. I was so proud when my work pleased her. Those hits of positive reinforcement were incredible, and so rare at this point in my life. The school initially required me to go to class once a week, pick up a packet of work, and turn it in by the end of the week. It doesn't sound like much, but that once a week commute was a struggle. I didn't have a vehicle at the time, so I usually had to bus it and walk, which took a couple of hours or so.

But the commute wasn't the only struggle. The fact that I was a walking target made it so much harder. I was clearly dressed as a gang member, and rivals were always on the lookout to catch someone slipping. Plus, I was young and that made people think they could mess with me. I can't tell you how many times I was in a fight after a car would pass by and notice me. I'd get into scuffles on the bus ride. But I didn't let that stop me from finishing school. I finished high school with my diploma after earning 220 credits. Little did I know that this piece of paper would be the key to getting an opportunity that would change my life in a positive manner forever.

CHAPTER 9

While I was attempting to attend school once a week, the block on 58th Street stayed hot and active between dealing with our rivals and law enforcement on the prowl. It was the weekend, so I headed to the hood once again. I was probably 12 or 13 now, and it was time to carry out my first mission. It was my chance to meet my rivals on the other side of the tracks.

Feuding with rivals happens for so many reasons. We fought over territory, money, power, respect, girls, and to get revenge for a previous slight. Sometimes it'd been going back and forth for a while, and you didn't want to be the one to end it. It's like a game of cat and mouse. Some of the feuding has gone on for years. The F13 gang is extremely territorial and defends its turf by any means necessary. Florence was our house and anyone who didn't respect the hood suffered the consequences. They hit something of Florencia's, we hit five of theirs, and on and on it went. A never-ending, vicious cycle. Rivaling over territory was a big deal. The more territory a gang occupies, the more ground you have to conduct gang business, which in turn means more money can be made.

I sat on the passenger's side of a "borrowed" car, and my homeboy Tristone was on the driver's side. I didn't know him very well. I had seen him around, but this was the first time we had actually met. There were two other cars parked in front of us. The first wave took off, and we were supposed to be in the third wave. Our job was to get there, take care of business, and get right back to 58th. Minutes later, the second wave headed out. Then a homeboy in the car behind us brings over a .22 caliber rifle with an extended banana clip and hands it to me. And when I say extended, I mean I've never seen a clip that long on a rifle before or since. The homie started to explain where we needed to go, what needed to be done, and then he headed back to his car.

I looked over at the homeboy Tristone and he looked as if he was scared. In my mind I was like what the fuck is wrong with this fool? He was starting to make me nervous. My heart started to beat a little faster. I think it was just fear of the unknown. My palms started getting sweaty. I could feel the adrenaline rush moving through me. I put the rifle on the left side of my leg and he freaked out. He told me to put that shit on my other side. So, I put it on the right side of my leg. I finally asked him what his problem was. He told me he just got out of the joint last week. So he was fresh out from serving time and on parole. That explained his nerves, but it didn't make me feel any better about going on this mission with him.

Moments later, the same homeboy from behind us came back and poked his head in the car. He took the rifle and said, "the boys are too hot, ese," and he waved the police scanner in his hand to demonstrate what he meant. He said we couldn't afford to lose the rifle. It was just too likely we'd get picked up by the cops. When I remember it now, I think fuck the rifle, what about us? I guess we were more disposable than a strap. I felt a sense of relief but I was also disappointed because my opportunity to put in work for the hood vanished as quickly as it came. The adrenaline rush went from 1-100 and now I was back to a 1. But I knew there would be many more opportunities.

Being posted up on 58th Street was risky business for the Malditos. We were easy access for an ambush from our rivals or to be busted by the cops. 58th Street was a wide-open, short block that ran east-west in between two major cross streets, Compton Avenue and Makee Avenue. There was an alleyway that ran north-south in between both streets. It provided easy, 4-way access to us in a vehicle at any time. Rivals usually drove by on Compton Ave and could shoot at us from there, but sometimes they got brave and would approach from the alleyway. Law enforcement could come at us from all angles, but rarely did so. The evidence of years of warfare with our rivals showed up as bullet holes in the walls of nearby apartments and along every surface in sight. One night we were caught slipping, totally unprepared and unaware, and it cost us a few homies catching bullets.

It was a Friday night, and the block was active. We were all hyped up because we had been feuding hard with rivals across the train tracks and we were all ready for war. Normally we're on high alert, looking at every car that passes, but from time to time we got caught slippin' as we let our guard down. A small pick-up truck was coming in hot off of Compton Ave onto 58th. It all happened so fast, yet felt incredibly slow.

Lil Sleepy was one of several homies who had just arrived to the hood a few minutes before the truck came at us. All of a sudden, we heard a small caliber gun going off. It sounded like it was coming from the back of the truck. Most of the homeboys scattered and managed to not get hit. Others weren't so lucky. Lil Sleepy told me later he looked over his shoulder and to his right, with his back turned to the truck. He remembers seeing a flash and then hearing the gun shots. He fell down and forward, but didn't know why. After we heard the initial shots, it sounded like a loud, sawed-off shotgun started going off from the back of the truck. Several homeboys got shot that day, including Sleepy. But Sleepy didn't know it yet. He didn't realize he'd been shot, because .22 caliber bullets tend to travel in your body instead of entering and exiting.

Once the truck got off its rounds and left, Lil Sleepy was approached by several of the homeboys. He started to feel a burning sensation and was short of breath. He'd been shot in the back, but no one had figured that out yet. All the homeboys attended to him and tried to make sure he was okay. That's when someone saw the bullet hole on the right side of his lower back. Lil Sleepy remembers thinking that was it. He was done and his life was over. He got taken to the hospital along with several other homies that were hit. He suffered a collapsed lung, damaged liver, and has a nice-sized zipper, or scar, as a souvenir on his back.

Lil Sleepy was 16 years old when he was shot in 1990. That night, his mom thought he was at home, asleep in his bed where he was supposed to be. He snuck out of the house once his mother turned in for the night. You can only imagine how she felt when she got the phone call that her son had been shot. She still thought he was safe, asleep in her house. We didn't have the cell phones and technology to keep track of kids like we do now. Lil Sleepy is one of the lucky few to survive.

It was around this time that the Malditos moved from hanging out on 58th to 59th Street. The quick access to us on 58th Street had made us targets. There were too many avenues for attack, making us easy marks. Too many homies were getting shot and busted by the cops on 58th. 59th Street was a whole other deal and would open up a brand new world for us.

When we moved to 59th Street, it was like a new beginning for the Malditos. It was also a strategic move for drug sales and gang business, because it made the Malditos less accessible to other gangs and law enforcement. The eleven hundred block of 59th Street is a street between Central Avenue and Hooper Avenue in the Florence-Firestone district. The homies quickly set up shop and began to heavily engage in drug sales and gang activity there. Business on 59th Street was a 24/7 operation. Safe houses were rented by the homies and used to slang drugs and hide from the police when they came looking for us. The drug of choice was crack cocaine. Crack in the 90's sold like hot tortillas. It was easy to manufacture because it could be made in the kitchen of a safe house, and so easy to sell because it was extremely addictive. Most of the buyer traffic came from Central Avenue and exited onto Hooper Avenue.

59th Street used to be a quiet, residential street where the locals could chill and relax in their front yards. Unfortunately for them, F13 Malditos invaded the block and imprisoned the residents in their own homes. Gone were the days kids could play outside or someone could walk their dog. The Malditos would sometimes see residents running just to get to their car, even during the day.

The Malditos invaded the block deep and kicked back on the street to sell crack and handle gang business. Sometimes we would be hanging out about 60 heads deep, at all hours any day of the week. There were several houses that the homies lived in, so we chilled outside those safe houses. The landlords that rented to us didn't give a shit about screening us to move in. They were only worried about the rent being paid on time, which was easy with the profits from crack sales. Most of our customers came from out of town. Some came from as far as Long Beach and even from the Valley. Customers could literally walk or drive up on 59th Street like it was an all-hours drive thru. F13 Malditos were in total control.

All the lights were shot out, so the dark street could easily hide us when the police or rivals would try to roll through looking to hassle us. Some of the homeboys even resorted to stealing and breaking into cars on the block and further terrorizing the residents. This eventually became a big no-no among the Malditos and we checked anyone who was caught doing so. "Getting checked" meant you took a royal ass beating by several homies at a time for breaking a rule. It's almost as if you were getting jumped into the gang all over again.

59th Street was long and gave us more territory than 58th ever had. We all hung out, mostly dead center on the block. Every time I showed up there was always something going on – a dice game, the homeboys slanging, music on, girls visiting, street boxing, and much more. There was constantly some activity and someone was always there. And through it all, the ghetto bird would be in the air, watching. The police would roll through once in a blue moon to say hello. They kept us on our toes, but if they didn't find any guns or drugs, we were good to go. The police raided several safe houses in the hood over time, but the homies were released shortly after and came back to do the same ol' shit on the same ol' block. The hood was always tagged up "Florencia 13 Malditos", claiming our territory. The local residents had to just sit back and watch all of this happen. It became the norm for them. I imagine now they were too scared and didn't want to antagonize us.

Soon, we noticed the police watching us closer. We caught wind that they were surveilling us. Patrols increased, undercovers were busting Malditos, and they even rolled up on bikes once or twice. They set up a portable police station. The block was hot then. So, most of us stayed away for a bit. After some time passed and things cooled off, we started everything back up on the block. It was beyond run down by this point with graffiti, trash, no lights, no grass, drug buys, and people openly pissing on the street. It was truly ghetto fabulous.

Then the police and the city of LA decided they were going to do something unprecedented. They changed 59th to a one way street. The goal was to disrupt the flow of drug traffic, so it moved opposite to the route our customers travelled. The police would just park at the end of the block, wait for the buys to happen, and then rough up the buyer right on the spot. This was a historic decision in Los Angeles, because a street direction change had never been used to upset gang or drug activity. This slowed down operations for F13 Malditos in the area for a bit, but as with everything, there was always another way. We just put plans B and C into motion.

One of the ways we worked around it was to have our customers park on the next block over. They'd pull up in front of a homie's house and walk through the driveway to a hole we cut in the fence. Then they'd be on

59th Street, buy their merchandise, and keep it moving. The 1st and 15th of the month were always the busiest in crack sales. That's when welfare checks and food stamps were issued. Instead of using their government assistance for rent and living expenses, crack heads and users would buy crack with it. That's how insanely addictive this stuff was. They would gladly exchange 300 dollars worth of food stamps for 20 dollars of crack. They would rather starve just so they could get another hit of that rock. Eventually the Malditos expanded to other streets nearby. 57th and 68th Street were soon added to our territory on top of 59th and our original home, 58th Street. The Malditos were on the move, and swallowing up as much terrain as we could.

CHAPTER 10

Flashbacks from the hood aren't rare. It's not uncommon for me to wake up disturbed, covered in sweat and thinking about the past. Sometimes when I daydream, random moments from those days will come back to me. I often wonder what the hell I was thinking back then, and to this day I wonder how I made it out alive. I looked over my shoulder for many years after I left the hood. Part of me didn't think I'd have a future, and expected to spend the rest of my life in prison.

I don't really know how I escaped getting strung out on drugs like so many of the other homeboys did. The very drugs that were sold by the Malditos, were the same drugs that destroyed homies all around me. I remember the eerie feeling of seeing homies fresh out of the joint on swoll status, all fit, muscular, and healthy, only to have their cheek bones showing within months of being released. They looked gaunt and sick because they were strung out on drugs. I recall several pregnant ladies rolling up and begging for crumbs of crack. Crack is the devil. The crack epidemic in the 90's destroyed so many lives and the neighborhood overall. I'll never forget the devastation it caused in our community that was already ravaged by gang warfare and poverty.

Not all of my flashbacks are so dark, though. There are warm memories, and things that still make me smile. You might wonder what we ate throughout the day on the block, since gang business was a 24/7 operation. It was hard to get away because that meant you missed out on money-making opportunities. Time was money. Local street food vendors were aware and took full advantage. But we came up with some real hood "gourmet" meals, some of which I still crave. The elote man or woman would come through with a huge pot full of warm, fresh corn-on-a-stick in a shopping cart. But this was no ordinary corn. The elote vendor would pull an ear from the hot pot, place it on a stick, paste it with butter, salt, pepper, lime juice, chili powder, and even some Tapatio sauce and then sprinkle cheese on it. It was incredible. The tamale vendor would roll through in the same fashion. Shopping cart with a pot full of hot tamales of all flavors, chicken and pork with green or red sauce, a dulce or sweet option, and beef as well. Pork tamales with green sauce would literally melt in my mouth and was my absolute favorite.

I can't forget about the ice cream truck that would come through as well. Let me tell you, ice cream wasn't the only thing they sold. I always asked for a bag of Frito Lays, opened up and covered with chili meat and beans, topped with nacho cheese and a plastic spoon to scarf it all down. That shit was bomb. Absolutely delicious. They would also sell Cup of Noodles already hot and prepared with lime juice, hot sauce, Frito Lay chips inside and Corn Nuts or pork rinds on the side.

A truck came through daily with fresh fruit, veggies, munchies, and everything else from candy bars to soda. It was like a convenience store on wheels. My favorite treat was the Mexican sweet bread. If you have never tried conchas, you haven't lived. You're totally missing out and need to get your life together! Also, my homeboy Flaco's mom would buy snacks and food in bulk and sell it out of her house 24 hours a day. She made a killing on sales from us. I have to admire how smart and opportunistic she was.

Once Downer and Gato got busted and were doing time, I began to hang with my boy, my ride or die, my dawg, my partner in crime, Lil Man. He is still my best friend. He and I were connected at the hip in the hood. When I was broke and didn't have a dollar to my name, he would feed me. He picked me up and never charged me gas money, but only because I didn't have any. Once I started making money and became hood-rich, I was greedy and tight-fisted. I never offered to repay him for gas money or treated him when we got something to eat. He still gives me a hard time about that. I hadn't learned yet that sharing is caring, and I'd never had access to that kind of money. I wanted to keep it all to myself and saved it for my first car. I was still a kid and immature, and didn't think to repay his generosity.

We were always together and have stuck by each other through thick and thin. When we get together now, we reminisce about the hood days and always go back to how grateful we are that we're still alive. This man has not only been a friend to me but acted as a father to me as well. He has welcomed me into his beautiful family and vice versa. He's the pickiest eater I know, and has the biggest heart on earth. And man does this old man have a left hook on him. He also has no fear and would do anything for his friends, family, and the hood. When we were young, he always volunteered me for fights, so I too could sharpen my street fighting skills. I'm grateful for it, because he prepared me well for fights with rivals over the years. I wish the knuckle in my right hand wasn't MIA because of him, but Lil Man and I will ride together till the wheels fall off!

It was late one night, sometime after midnight. Me, Lil Man, and three of the homies were chilling on the block. All four of us were hanging in front of one of the homie's safe houses. We were all standing on the sidewalk in line with the driveway, just shooting the shit and making some money. I looked to my left and could see the homeboy Smokey riding a beach cruiser in our direction. He was about five houses down from us, but easy to recognize because he was a tall, lanky homie.

It was then I noticed a car moving towards us in the same direction and coming pretty fast. This put us on high alert, but it was too late to intervene. The car stopped in the middle of the street and started shooting at Smokey. I recognized the sound of an AK-47 assault rifle just unloading the clip. It happened so fast and we could see Smokey fall to the ground with his bike. We didn't know if he was dead or alive. Then the car burned rubber until they were stopped at angle, almost directly in front of us. They started to spray the fuck out of us. It happened so fast, yet time just slowed to a crawl. The gunshots rang out loud and powerful in my ears. My homeboy next to me pulled out his heat and began to fire back as the rest of us ran away.

I remember turning around to run away down the driveway. I was running as fast as I could when I felt one of the bullets graze my ear. I fell to the ground, scraping my hands, knees, and chin. I picked myself up and jumped the fence into the next yard over. Only one of us caught a bullet that night and by the grace of God the homeboy survived. He got shot in the hand and recovered quickly. The fact that there was minimal damage with so many bullets fired told me that the shooter was probably an inexperienced young kid that was told to take care of business. No doubt in my mind the man above was looking out for us.

CHAPTER 11

I had a spray can in my ride, ready to strike up some graffiti on a wall with big F13 block letters. I wanted everyone to see this hit-up. I had already designed it in my mind, so I wanted it in a high traffic area. Finally, I narrowed it down to the neighborhood liquor store where all the homeboys bought their booze to get the weekend started.

I was known to have some of the best gang-style graffiti letters in all of Florencia. So much so that all the other cliques began to copy my style, including our rivals. At any given time, the homies from every clique in Florencia would be at this particular store, stocking up on alcohol. The liquor store was located on the corner of Florence and Hooper Avenue. I remember we drove over there from 59th Street with my boy Lil Man and the homeboy Spike. The store had a long, clean wall on the Hooper Avenue side that was just waiting for me to mark our territory.

It was early evening as I started to strike up in block letters, stretching above my head as high as I could. I wrote: F13 MDS Chico, Lil Man, Spike. As soon as I finished, the police rolled up on me. They jumped out of their cars with their guns drawn and asked me not to move. They shouted at me to drop the spray can, and put my hands behind my head. Then one of the police officers came up behind me and handcuffed me. He grabbed me from behind by both arms, and slammed me onto the hood of his car. Then he pushed my face sideways into metal hot enough to burn my skin.

He kicked my feet apart and started to shake me down for weapons and contraband. The other officer asked me for my ID and I responded that I didn't have one. Then he asked me how old I was and wanted to know why I had so much cash in my pocket. I had a wad of ones, fives, and ten dollar bills from hustling in the hood. I responded by saying that I was sixteen years old and that I worked construction with my uncle. He looked at me and said, "Bullshit. You're older than that and we know where this money comes from. You've got to be about 20 years old." I've always looked older than advertised.

The police officer proceeded to tell me that if I didn't cross out the graffiti that he would take me to jail. I told him fuck no, I wasn't crossing it out. Go ahead and take me to jail. So, they threw me in the back seat, and we all went to the new county jail in Lynwood. I was booked on April 7th, 1994, at the age of 16. I remember that day clearly, because it was my boy Lil Man's birthday.

I had never been arrested before. They began to inprocess me as soon as I got to the Lynwood police station. I told them my name and my social security number. I had never been in trouble before, so there was no record of me in the system. Before they took me in, the cops had ripped my shirt off, removed my shoes, and threatened to take me to Watts. It was on the other side of the tracks, in F13's rival's territory. If they had made good on that threat, I could have been hurt, or even killed just for being there. This was a standard scare tactic that the cops used on homeboys.

During inprocessing I was asked multiple questions by one of the clerks including what gang I was from and what my street name was. I proudly said South Central La Florencia 13 Los Malditos, and they call me Chico. The lady made the comment that my homeboys were always in trouble and often got to come meet her. Then it was fingerprints on some fancy machine followed by my mug shot. Before I was taken to the holding cell, the deputies searched me. I was asked to strip down naked, bend over, and grab my ankles. Then I had to spread my ass cheeks and cough three times. After that I was asked to grab my dick, and lift up my nut sack. I was mortified. I'm sure there's a legitimate reason for every part of this in-processing dance, but it was embarrassing and degrading. When I reflect on it now, I know there are consequences for defacing someone's property, and my first stint in jail could have been much worse.

Once my in-processing was done, I was taken to the holding cell. When I walked in, I noticed several gang members hanging around the entrance. I announced my hood as soon as I walked in by saying, "Was up fool, Florencia 13 Los Malditos" to this ese that had XV3 tatted on the front of his neck. The mix of Roman numerals and regular numbers told me he was from 18th Street, a rival gang of F13. Before I could take another breath, I felt two heavy ass hands grab me from behind and force me into the corner. It shook me how easily he overpowered me, but he was a big boy. I strained to look up and back at him. I recognized him as one of the older homies from Florence, from the Jokers clique. I don't remember his hood name, but I often saw him at Florence parties. He shook me up hard and asked what the fuck I thought I was doing. He told me that this ain't no place to be banging on South Siders. We all stick together in here.

Initially I was confused, but I started to remember all the talk from my homies who had been busted before about the gang rules in county, state, and federal prisons. It totally slipped my mind that gang banging against our own was against the code we followed. It didn't matter if they were a hood rival or not. Part of the county jail politics is that we remained segregated. Sureños all stick together no matter what hood they're from. African Americans, Asians, Caucasians, and Paisas - everyone sticks within their own group and lives by set rules as well. The segregation is just a part of prison politics. If someone crosses a line, you're dealt with by your own group. If you know about or witness someone crossing the line, you deal with them or wait to be dealt with yourself. Pick your poison. The older homie said no more and he clearly wanted me to let him be. I'm not sure what the homie was busted for but he laid down and crashed out. I recognized my mistake, and sat to wait for whatever came next.

I was finally escorted to my cell. I didn't receive any linen and the door just slammed shut behind me. There were two hard metal bunks, one on bottom and one on top. I didn't have a cellmate, so at least there was that. As I lay there, I took in the bleak, cold cell. There was a small window that let you peek outside. It was cold as fuck, so all I could do was ball up as tight as I could. They had given me an oversized jail jumpsuit, but it wasn't enough to keep me warm. The cold was overwhelming and soon my body started to shake. Hours passed before I finally fell asleep.

They woke me up for chow out in the lounge area. When I came to, I felt like an iceberg. My feet, hands, and ears were frozen, my throat was sore, and my nose was running. I don't really remember what food was served, but I know for sure it didn't taste good. An ese from the Compton Varrio 70's gang came to sit down with me. We made small talk and kept it moving. Another day passed.

I remember I was called out to what looked like a control center and was asked by a deputy how old I was. I told him I was sixteen. He asked me why I was there and I said for striking up on a wall. He laughed and asked me if I told the arresting officer my age and I said yes. The next thing

I knew, I was escorted to this empty room with just a single chair in it. The walls were bright white. I sat there for what seemed like an eternity. I'm sure it was at least a few hours.

What I didn't know was that my mother had been in contact with my best friend trying to find me. It was normal for me to stay out for days or even weeks at a time, so she was used to me just disappearing. I'm glad she was paying attention this time. They told me my mother called the jailhouse looking for me. Finally, a deputy came in and asked me again how old I was. I told him and then he asked me to call my mother, who was expecting to hear from me. The deputies finally escorted me home, and released me to my mother after she produced my birth certificate.

A few weeks after my release, I received a summons to appear before a judge in court. My mother accompanied me to the court house, which was right outside of downtown Los Angeles. I felt totally lame wearing some tight ass pants with a button-down shirt and tie that my moms bought from Goodwill. I had never worn anything like it before, but did so to look presentable in front of the judge. I was amazed by how much gang graffiti was in the elevator as we made our way up to a higher floor. My mom stepped out of the elevator before I did. I took a moment to graffiti F13 MDS using the marker I always carried with me. My mother walked back to see what the hold up was and she was infuriated! But I couldn't help myself.

We sat down in the courtroom. There were several guys in front of me waiting to see the judge. Every single one of them got called in front of the judge and walked out in cuffs. They were all taken into custody. Then they called me up to the court table next to the public defender. A few things were said, but the only thing I really remembered was that the judge said he was sentencing me to 120 days in the LA County Jail. I responded, "Let's go, take me!" Then my mother stood up behind me in the crowd and yelled really loud, "No, no, you can't take him to jail, he's only sixteen years old! You can't do this again!"

Everyone in the courtroom started looking around lost and confused. I stood up, put my hands out and told them to take me. Told them not to listen to her. I was ready to earn my stripes in the LA County Jail. My mother kept repeating over and over that my son is only 16, you can't take him. Finally, the bailiff came over as my mother offered him my birth certificate. After some discussion, the judge dismissed me from the courtroom and let me know I would be hearing from a probation officer at some point. I received my letter in the mail several days later, telling me it was time to report. When I did, the probation officer was surprised by my story. He even asked me why I didn't sue the Los Angeles County Sheriff's Department.

As I look back at this time in my life, I wonder what would have happened if my mother hadn't stood up for me in that courtroom. I would have been in the Los Angeles County Jail and there's no doubt in my mind I would have picked up a case or two while I was in there. I still wanted to make a name for myself, and an easy way to do that would be to commit other crimes while I was doing time, and extend my stay. Sometimes you got orders, but I was thirsty for blood and wanted to earn my stripes, so who knows what I would have done. I was a follower, and a loyal one at that. I have no doubt that I would have put in work or taken care of business if ordered to do so by higher echelon homies. My mom saved me that day, and I'm grateful she did. Thanks to her, I still had a chance at a better future.

CHAPTER 12

It was the weekend in the hood and it was active as usual on 59th Street. It was a ritual that when the weekend came, a handful of homies would walk down the street to the corner of 59th and Central Ave to strike up the wall with a spray can or two. We wanted all the traffic and onlookers to see it, and more importantly, we wanted our rivals to see it. As one of the homeboys was getting ready to strike up on the wall, a four-door unmarked car stopped right in front of us. A middle-aged woman in civilian clothes got out with her gun pointed dead at us, showed us her badge with the other hand, and screamed at us to stop. She said, "Don't fucking move!"

I walked right up to her car and I told her to get the fuck out of here. I could see she was scared. Her eyes gave her away and I didn't blame her. All my homies were right across the street, watching the scene unfold. They all had heat in their waistbands. The numbers were not in her favor. She got back in her car and drove away without anyone getting hurt. My guess is she was on her way home from work or off duty and she regretted stopping almost as soon as she'd done it. Something in my gut told me to let it be and head back to 59th.

I started walking back down to 59th Street, where more of the homies were chilling. There was a crowd of girls hanging on the sidewalk, wearing daisy duke shorts and looking fine as hell. They rolled up in a nice four-door Honda Accord, a car that you didn't normally see in the hood. I approached one of the girls and asked her what a pretty young lady like her was doing in South Central. She said that she and her friends had heard about the parties the Florence boys threw and they wanted to check it out. They were from the Valley. We chatted them up for a while before they hopped in their car, getting ready to leave for the next neighborhood party.

Their car was facing east towards Hooper Avenue. I came around to the driver's side of the car so I could talk to the girl some more before they took off. We kept chatting and I was getting ready to ask for her number. I looked over my right shoulder and noticed my best friend Lil Man shooting dice with the homeboy Poncho. I was a skilled and lucky dice player myself, and normally would have been playing, but the girls had kept me occupied. Then I looked over my left shoulder and saw what appeared to be a small Toyota pick-up truck heading towards us from the west on 59th Street. Normally we were on high alert, ready for rivals rolling through or the cops.

The truck was heading our way, super slow, and somehow no one thought anything of it. Everyone was too occupied. I put my head into the girl's car so I could ask her for her number. She gave it to me without hesitation. Then I asked her for a kiss and got that too. The next thing I knew, I heard what sounded like a cap gun going off. I looked back and could see the Toyota truck taking off, followed by a loud scream that came from across the street. Immediately I ran over to Lil Man and Poncho and could see Poncho was on his back with his legs up under him.

Then all hell broke loose. Everyone was in disbelief because no one came through our turf and left untouched. We were caught slipping. We were all distracted and weren't ready for the attack. The worst part was that nobody jumped in their cars and chased them down until the truck made a right going north on Central Ave. The homeboy Poncho was screaming at the top of his lungs. He was in so much pain and was distraught. It's a scream I will never forget. "My son…my son. I want to see my son." Poncho had a newborn baby at home.

The homeboy Big Cyco, rest in peace, was furious that no one jumped in their cars and chased the truck down. The homie Angel R.I.P. and his car were parked near where Poncho was shot. It was a '64 Impala with a nice candy coat paint job and Dayton wire wheels. I watched as Cyco R.I.P. jumped on the hood of the car and began to smash the windshield with his foot out of pure rage. The homeboy Poncho was starting to turn pale and the bullet wound on his back was leaking blood. The homeboy Cyco R.I.P. came over and pulled Poncho's legs out from under him, not knowing it would cause more damage. It was taking longer than normal for the ambulance to arrive. My understanding has always been that the ambulance couldn't arrive until the cops deemed it safe for them. A few of the homeboys were keeping Poncho warm and trying to keep him calm.

Then finally, the homies started jumping into cars and heading in the direction where we knew the truck came from. We were feuding hard with a rival on the other side of the tracks at the time. I jumped in a car with another homeboy and headed to Poncho's house to notify his baby's momma about the incident and also to grab my strap. When we got there, his baby momma was sleeping. We pounded on the door and the windows and she finally opened up. We let her know that Poncho had been shot on 59th Street. I also asked her if I could grab my heat, since I had Poncho hold it for me at his house. She got dressed, grabbed the baby, and headed to 59th Street.

My homie and I ran back to the car and headed over to the other side of the tracks. Let's just say there were a lot of fireworks in the air that night. After things died down, we headed back to 59th Street. The homie parked and we got out of the car. We found out that the ambulance took Poncho to Killer King Hospital a.k.a. Martin Luther King Jr. Community Hospital in Willowbrook. They called it Killer King because a lot of gang-bangers got taken there and, as a county hospital, they couldn't be turned away. But that didn't stop more than a few of them from dying in the lobby, waiting to be seen by a doctor. No disrespect to the current hospital, since the old Killer King was shut down in 2007 for all the incidents that gave it it's dark moniker. I visited several homies who were shot and taken there, not just Poncho.

Within minutes of parking the car on 59th, we could hear the ghetto bird coming and then we saw the cops turning the corner and flying towards us. All the homeboys started scrambling away, mostly into the safe houses, but I ended up running into a resident's driveway where several cars were parked. As I was running, I pulled my heat from my waist band and chucked it up on the roof of a nearby house. I slid under a car and just laid there for what seemed like forever. The other two cars parked in the drive were sheltering two more of my homeboys. I could hear the ghetto bird circling the hood and cops walking all around us. For whatever reason, and by the grace of God, they didn't come close enough to find us.

I could tell that the car I was under had just been parked because it was hot as hell under there and I could feel the oil start to drip down my face. I was pissed, but nervous as fuck too. I wasn't ready to go to jail that night for any reason. It seemed like a couple of hours passed before the activity around us died down and we couldn't hear any more commotion. The other two homies and I crawled out from under the cars, dirty as fuck. We soon found out that while Poncho was in bad shape, he had lived to see another day. A .22 caliber bullet traveled up his spine and unfortunately left him paralyzed for the rest of his life. He had to go through numerous surgeries and countless therapy sessions. But thankfully he is still here and got to see his son grow up and make a wonderful life for himself.

PHOTO GALLERY

A SNAPSHOT OF THE HOMIE "CUETE'S"
SOUTH SIDE FLORENCIA 13 TERMITES TATTOO.

F13 MALDITOS POSTED UP IN
SOUTH CENTRAL LOS ANGELES.

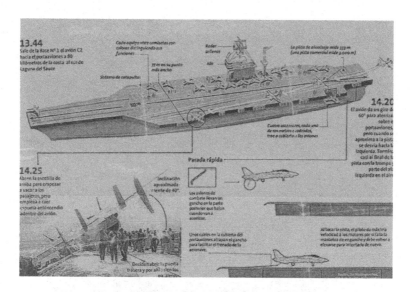

A NEWS CLIP OF THE AIRCRAFT FILLED WITH VIPS THAT NEARLY MADE ITS WAY INTO THE OCEAN.

MY SISTER LISA FLASHING HER GANG SIGN ALONGSIDE HER HOMEGIRLS FROM CF 13.

ME POSTED UP ON 59 STREET. IT WAS JUST ANOTHER DAY AT THE OFFICE.

ME IN MY UNITED STATES NAVY "MASTER JEFE" CHOKER WHITES UNIFORM.

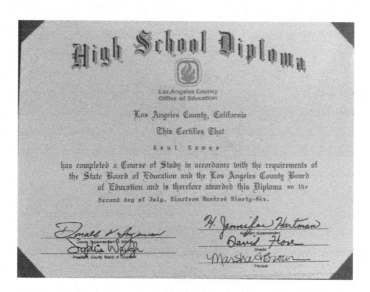

THE HIGH SCHOOL DIPLOMA THAT GAVE ME AN OPPORTUNITY TO JOIN THE UNITED STATES NAVY.

ME THE DAY I VISITED MY TIA ROSA'S HOUSE
WITH MY FACE TATTOOS COVERED UP OUT OF RESPECT FOR HER HOME OF RESIDENCE.

MY RIGHT OUTER LOWER LEG TATTOOS.
NIKE CORTEZ SNEAKERS THAT I WORE DURING MY ADVENTURES IN THE HOOD, RAIDER NATION FOR MY FAVORITE
FOOTBALL TEAM, AND SC LOGO FOR SOUTH CENTRAL, SO CAL, AND SOUTHERN CALIFORNIA TROJANS FOOTBALL TEAM.

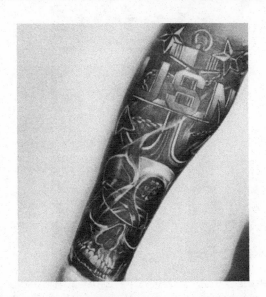

TATTOO ON MY LOWER LEFT ARM OF A "MASTER JEFE" ANCHOR AND SKULL.

MY SON RAULITO GETTING BELTED UP BY HIS MOTHER FOR A TAEKWONDO SESSION.

MY MENTEE "STAFO" AND I POSTED UP POST HIS COMMISSIONING CEREMONY.

F13 MALDITOS POSTED UP DURING THE GANG PEACE TREATY IN B13 TERRITORY POST OUR FOOTBALL GAME.

ME RUNNING THE HOT CHOCOLATE 15K IN SEATTLE WASHINGTON ON A COLD AND RAINY DAY.

IT WAS AN HONOR TO SERVE AS A NAVY SENIOR CHIEF SELECTION BOARD MEMBER.

ME (CHICO - TOP RIGHT), MY BEST FRIEND (LIL MAN – BOTTOM MIDDLE) POSTED UP DRINKING BUDWEISER BEER.

ME (CHICO - FAR LEFT), LIL MAN, LIL CYCO R.I.P, AND KOOPA R.I.P.

LET'S JUST SAY I WAS IN A ZONE BACK THERE.

THE DAY I WAS PROMOTED TO "MASTER JEFE".

RUNNING UP HILL ON THE LAST SEVERAL MILES OF THE SAN DIEGO ROCK N ROLL MARATHON.
THE YOUNG LADY TO MY LEFT ASKED ME TO MOTIVATE HER UP THE HILL. LITTLE DID SHE KNOW SHE MOTIVATED ME.

THE FACES SHOWN ARE ME
(CHICO - BOTTOM, KOOPA R.I.P. – TOP LEFT, TORO R.I.P., AND PONCHITO PRIOR TO BEING PARALYZED.

THE HOMIE (SMOKEY –FAR LEFT, ME CHICO, LIL MAN, AND DIABLO R.I.P.)

THE FACES SHOWN ARE LIL SLEEPY AND BIG POISON POSTED UP ON 58 STREET.

F13 MALDITOS POSTED UP ON 59 STREET. FACES SHOWN TORO R.I.P., ME CHICO, LIL MAN, AND PONCHITO.

ME, LIL MAN, AND DOWNER ON FAR RIGHT.

THE HOMIES PLAYING FOOTBALL AGAINST B13 GANG DURING GANG PEACE TREATY.

DOWNER DOING TIME IN CALIFORNIA YOUTH AUTHORITY.

WALL ARTWORK ON 58 STREET.

WALL ARTWORK ON 58 STREET AND THE HOMIES POSTED UP.

THE HOMIES POSTED UP IN BETHUNE PARK IN SOUTH CENTRAL LOS ANGELES IN THE FLORENCE DISTRICT –
TOP MIDDLE – STRANGER, TOP RIGHT – YUCK R.I.P.,
BOTTOM LEFT TO RIGHT – KOOPA R.I.P., BIG POISON, LIL SLEEPY, ME CHICO, AND LIL MAN.

ME AND MY MENTOR BALT ON LIBERTY IN BALTIMORE MARYLAND.

JUST FINISHED RUNNING 26.2 MILES IN SAN DIEGO CALIFORNIA.

I WAS SO WEAK POST THE MARATHON I WAS STRUGGLING TO OPEN THE GATORADE BOTTLE.

MY SISTER AND I (2-3 YEARS OLD). RUNNING JOKE WAS WE WERE TWIN SISTERS.

ME AT THE VERY TOP, MY MENTEE GEORGE FIERROS
BOTTOM LEFT, AND MY MENTOR MASTER JEFE (RETIRED) DREW CHINLOY ONBOARD THE MIGHTY WARSHIP NIMITZ.

LIL SLEEPY TOP LEFT, AND LIL MAN IN THE MIDDLE.

ME CHILLING AT FREEMONT HIGH SCHOOL IN SOUTH CENTRAL LOS ANGELES

MY MENTEE GEORGE FIERROS AND I ON THE FLIGHT DECK OF THE MIGHTY WARSHIP NIMITZ.

AIR DEPARTMENT CHIEFS ONBOARD THE MIGHTY WARSHIP NIMITZ 2017.
I'M IN THE MIDDLE SQUATTING DOWN IN MY ESE POSE.

LETS JUST SAY I WAS IN A ZONE BACK THERE.

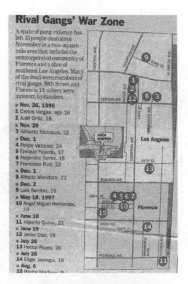

Rival Gangs' War Zone

A spate of gang violence has left 15 people dead since November in a two-square-mile area that includes the unincorporated community of Florence and a slice of southeast Los Angeles. Many of the dead were members of rival gangs, 38th Street and Florencia 13; others were innocent bystanders.

■ **Nov. 26, 1996**
1 Carlos Vargas, age 18
2 Juan Orbiz, 18
■ **Nov. 29**
3 Gilberto Mendoza, 22
■ **Dec. 1**
4 Felipe Vazquez, 24
5 Enrique Fajardo, 17
6 Alejandro Torrez, 15
7 Francisco Ruiz, 22
■ **Dec. 1**
8 Alfredo Mendoza, 22
■ **Dec. 2**
9 Luis Benitez, 15
■ **May 18, 1997**
10 Angel Miguel Hernandez, 19
■ **June 18**
11 Hipolito Quiroz, 21
■ **June 19**
12 Javier Diaz, 16
■ **July 25**
13 Hector Reyes, 28
■ **July 28**
14 Edgar Jauregui, 18
■ **Aug. 6**
15 Hector Martinez, 9

LOS ANGELES TIMES NEWS ARTICLE.
I COULD HAVE EASILY BEEN A VICTIM ALONGSIDE VICTIMS R.I.P. "4,5,6,7,."
A PAGE ON MY BEEPER SAVED ME.

MY BIG SIS LISA POSTED UP FLASHING HER GANG SIGN.

MY FIRST HALF MARATHON RACE BIB.

MY FATHER HARD AT WORK.

MY UNCLE MIGUEL AND I IN BARRIO LOGAN – SAN DIEGO CALIFORNIA.

MY FAMILY – FROM LEFT TO RIGHT,
TIO MIGUEL, COUSIN ROSA A.K.A. HUERA, TIA ROSA, COUSIN ERNESTO, AND COUSIN/COMPA MIKE

MY SAN DIEGO ROCK N' ROLL MARATHON BIB.

ME AND MY FAVORITE EAST COAST HUMANS CHRIS AND BRI!.

MY SON RAULITO AND I CHILLIN'.

MY ARRESTING GEAR CREW AND I ONBOARD THE MIGHTY WARSHIP REAGAN 2007.

BOOTCAMP DIVISION 341 PICTURE DAY 1998.

ME AND AIR DEPARTMENT CHIEFS ONBOARD THE MIGHTY WARSHIP NIMITZ 2017.

MY BEST FRIEND LIL MAN AND I POSTED UP ON 59 STREET.

MY BEST FRIEND LIL MAN AND I AT MY GOING AWAY FOR BOOTCAMP PARTY 1998.

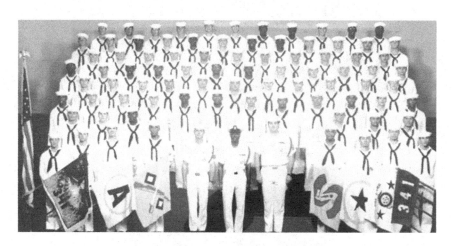

MY BOOTCAMP DIVISION 341 PICTURE.

MASTER JEFE IN DRESS BLUE UNIFORM.

ELOTE MAN.

PROUD OF BEING MEXICAN/AMERICAN.

WHILE I WAS STATIONED IN MONTEREY CALIFORNIA, I WAS SELECTED FOR PROMOTION TO SENIOR CHIEF. MY SAILORS DECIDED TO FOIL EVERY BIT OF MY OFFICE DOWN TO EVERY WIRE.

RAULTIO WAS SO HAPPY AT THE NASCAR RACE.

RAULITO AND I WATCHING THE NASCAR RACE.

THE HOMIES PRACTICING WALL ART ON 58 STREET.

8. APPLICANT		e. WITNESS		
(1) SIGNATURE	(2) DATE SIGNED (YYMMDD)	(1) TYPED OR PRINTED NAME	(2) RANK / GRADE	(3) SIGNATURE

SECTION VI - REMARKS (Specify item(s) being continued by item number. Continue on separate pages if necessary)

DD Form 369 sent to the following Agencies: Los Angeles Police Dept, Los Angeles County Sheriffs, California state Hwy Patrol.

980425: A COMMANDING OFFICER'S INTERVIEW REGARDING "OBJECTIONABLE TATTOO'S" WAS CONDUCTED ON 980425 AND THE APPLICANT, RAUL RUBEN RAMOS IS AUTHORIZED ENLISTMENT INTO THE U.S. NAVY NOTWITHSTANDING HIS TATTOS.

C. J. Ellis
C. J. ELLIS, CDR, USN
COMMANDING OFFICER
NAVCRUITDIST LOS ANGELES

	DD FORM 1966-4 ATTACHED (X one)	YES
		NO ☒

DD Form 1966/3, APR 94   PREVIOUS EDITION MAY BE USED.   S/N 0102-LF-018-9500   Page 2

THE WAIVER THAT ALLOWED ME TO SERVE AND SAVED MY LIFE.

USS MAKIN ISLAND AIR DEPARTMENT CHIEFS AND I.

I WAS ON THE FINAL STRETCH OF 26.2 MILES DURING THE SAN DIEGO ROCK N ROLL MARATHON.

ONE OF THE GREATEST DAYS OF MY CAREER.
I WAS PROMOTED TO CHIEF ONBOARD THE MIGHTY WARSHIP REAGAN 2008.

MY SISTER LISA AND I.

MY FATHER AND I.

RAULITO PRACTICING TAEKWONDO.

F13 MALDITOS POSTED UP.

RAULITO, EMILY AND I.

MY BEST FRIEND LIL MAN AND I.

MY MOTHER ALICIA.

BIG CYCO R.I.P. F13 MALDITOS

MY FATHER AND MOTHER WHEN THEY WERE FIRST DATING.

FROM LEFT TO RIGHT, ME, PONCHITO, SHADOW, AND LIL MAN.

TOP LEFT, BIG CRICKET R.I.P, BIG ROCKY, SMOKES, BOTTOM LEFT, SCOOBY AND CRICKET.
ALL OF THEM HAD STREET FIGHTING SKILLS LIKE NO OTHER.

THIS IS UNITED STATES MARINE ROB ALVISO WHO TWISTED MY ARM TO
GO ON A FREEZING COLD RUN WITH HIM IN NEWPORT RHODE ISLAND.

MELINDA AND HER BEAUTIFUL FAMILY.

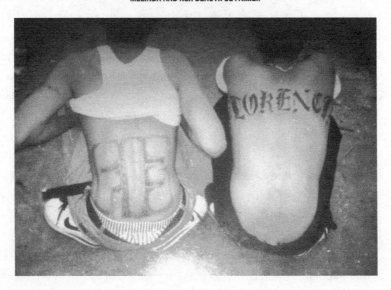

I WAS ABOUT 140 POUNDS SOAKING WET, 12 YEARS OLD WITH A FRESH "F13" BLOCK LETTER TATTOO ON MY BACK.

CHAPTER 13

I'll never forget the time I invited my first cousin, Mike, to the hood to hangout on 59th Street with me. I call him compa Mike, short for compadre. Mike is the son of Tio Miguel and my beloved Tia Rosa, the same tia that helped raise my father and took him in when he first came to the U.S. Compa Mike is a gentle giant, and when I first met him he stood about 6 feet 2 inches tall and weighed in at around 280 pounds. He was raised in Vallejo, a nice suburb up in northern California, along with my other cousins, his brother Ernesto and their sister Rosalva a.ka. Heura.

My Tia Rosa has the biggest heart and is one of the kindest people I know. I met them all when I was about 8 years old and they took me and my sister in with open arms. They have been there and supported me through untold trials and struggles. I have so much respect and love for them, that I covered the tattoos on my face before I entered their house. My tia's husband, Uncle Miguel, was the first man on this earth to put me to work and pay me some honest cash money. It was a lesson I didn't know I needed, but it struck such a sharp contrast to hustling I did in in the hood that I never forgot it. I was probably 12 years old when he put me to work in his yard, digging holes and painting his fence. At the end of the day he rewarded me with a stack of bills, and I can honestly say I'd never felt more proud or so accomplished as I did with that hard-earned, honest money sitting in my hand.

He may not have realized the gift he gave me that day, but it has stuck with me my whole life, and I've applied it in my career to make it to the top. He not only instilled a work ethic in me, but he modeled it as well. The lesson was to work hard, don't complain, and follow directions. If you could do those simple things, you'd be rewarded. You have to grind and just make shit happen. I'm eternally grateful for the guidance I so desperately needed and to Tio Miguel for showing me he was there for me.

Compa Mike takes after his amazing parents. He has supported me in so many ways and even baptized my daughter, Emily. He has taught me almost as much as Tia Rosa and Tio Miguel. Once, when Mike and his sister Huera came to visit me in Los Angeles, they took me to Red Lobster. I think I was 18 and I had never been to a restaurant before. Fast food, sure, but nothing "sit down" with waiters. I had no clue what to do when the waiter handed me a menu. I was so confused and couldn't figure out how to order. Mike schooled me down on the menu and explained how the whole restaurant thing worked. I felt like I was 5 years old again. This was a whole world I didn't even know existed, but I was so grateful that he walked me through it with minimal ribbing. I ordered my food and was shocked when my plate came. There was a huge, intact, red lobster just sitting there staring at me. I looked over at my compa and asked him how I was supposed to eat this thing? Mike and Huera laughed out loud. I flushed as red as that lobster, but I managed to eat it and it was absolutely delicious. I'd never had a meal like that before and I don't think any of us could forget that night. I'm thankful that I can now eat lobster and steak whenever I want, but that first lobster will always be the best one.

I thought a good payback for compa Mike since he laughed at me at Red Lobster would be to invite him to the hood on 59th Street that evening. Keep in mind that my compa lived in the burbs up in the hills of Vallejo and played with his high school band. He had never been exposed to the hardcore gang lifestyle. And he had never been to South Central LA.

It was a Friday night when I took Mike to the hood. I could see some fear in his eyes but also a gleam of excitement. He was intrigued by the unknown and part of him was ready to descend into my world. We rolled up to 59th Street and parked in front of all of the homies that were just chilling. My cousin stepped out of the passenger side of my car and of course, my biggest homeboy immediately stepped up to him. Big Cyco R.I.P. challenged him with a, "Where you from, ese?", asking what gang he was from. I probably should have been paying more attention, but I was distracted for a minute.

Completely unschooled on gang etiquette, my cousin said he was from northern Cali. That was the absolute wrong thing to say. My homeboy said, "What? Are you a Norteño?" He wanted to know if he was a northern Cali gangster. I immediately jumped in and told the homeboy to chill out, that he was my cousin and doesn't gangbang. Thankfully, that deescalated the situation and my homeboy let it go. But within minutes, loud gunshots started going off. At first, it seemed like they were coming from just down the street, so that put everyone, including my cousin, into a panic.

When we realized the gun shots were coming from the next block over, all of the homeboys started jumping in their cars to scope out the scene. Some just booked it over there on two feet. I made eye contact with Mike and I could see his discomfort and fear. His face had gone pale and I knew he had never witnessed anything like this. I told my cousin to stay put in the car and that I'd be right back. Once I got over to the next block, I realized it was a drive-by shooting. Someone shot up a homie's house, but luckily no one was home. We saw drive-by shootings as a cowardly move and they weren't tolerated. If we decided to get in a car with guns, we were expected to get out and take care of business. There were too many innocent bystanders getting caught in gang war crossfires from drive-bys and the higher echelon homies didn't like the heat we were getting from law enforcement.

After the drive-by mess, I thought we could rescue the night with some fun at a house party. I took my cousin and when we walked in you could barely move, it was so packed with homeboys. Mike found a safe spot in the corner and just stood there quietly, observing but still clearly uncomfortable. Meanwhile, I was on my own turf, far more at ease than I'd been in the restaurant that night. I was just talking to all the homies, shooting the shit, drinking my 40 ounce, while others were blowing smoke in the air. The music was banging and the dance floor opened up. The party had just begun and raged for hours. At the time, I didn't feel bad about that night, but I do now. I can put myself in his shoes and I feel terrible for not taking better care of him. Thank God we both walked away unscathed and I'm proud of my compa for surviving his night in South Central.

My Tia Rosa and her family are what I see when I close my eyes and envision a family. They're not perfect, but their flaws are perfect to me. They support and love one another and welcomed me with open arms. They provided me safe harbor when I needed it and loved me when I'm not sure I deserved it.

It was the middle of the day in the middle of summer, so it was sunny and hot in the hood. We got wind that there were some fools from a local gang that we normally got along with that were slanging crack out of a safe house. They set up shop without talking to the homies about it, which is not how we did business. One of the other homies and I were ordered to head over there to shake them up and have a serious talk with them. I was handed a chrome .45 caliber handgun, and my homeboy Dreamboy was armed with a TEC-9 semi-automatic pistol in case they wanted to get froggy.

We hopped in another homeboy's car with me in the back seat, and Dreamboy in the front. We drove several blocks away and cruised along about 5 mph with all three of us scoping out the scene. We made it all the way to the end of the block and saw nothing. So we hit the main street, Central Avenue. We circled the block several times, and with each round my palms got sweatier. My anxiety was super high. Not much was said between the three of us. I think maybe the third time around, we recognized the car in front of us. There were two heads in it. Central Avenue had heavy traffic going both directions, so we came to a stop. The car in front of us was only 20-30 feet away, ready to cross and head north on Central. I could see the tires had already started to turn that way when Dreamboy said, "Let's go and say hello." That was the call to get out of the car and have a chat with the two in the other vehicle.

I headed towards the driver's side of the car and Dreamboy, who was riding shotgun, moved to the passenger's side. He cocked back his heat and I took the safety off of mine just in case they wanted some of that smoke. We slowly approached the car that was still waiting to turn on Central Ave. My homeboy and I simultaneously tapped on both windows with the butt of our straps. I'll never forget the fear and shock in the driver's eyes when he saw me in his face with a gun in my hand. Then he looked over at my homeboy on the other side of his car and just froze. His passenger started reaching down for something by his feet and then I heard my homeboy scream, "My gun jammed! Fuck!"

The passenger was still reaching for his gun when the driver snapped out of it and the car suddenly burned rubber. They almost rammed into several other nearby cars but finally managed to take off untouched. It was then that I looked over Dreamboy's shoulder to the corner and saw an elderly lady with a young girl who may have been 8 years old. They were right behind Dreamboy, and had been getting ready to walk across the street. My heart dropped, thinking how close they had been to bullets flying. I felt some type of way. This little girl had her whole life ahead of her and our stupid actions could have ruined it. I was ashamed, thinking how everything could have changed in an instant for her or her caretaker if that gun hadn't jammed.

We ran back to the homie's car and he punched the pedal in reverse until we were on Hooper Avenue and had made it back to a safe house in the hood. We couldn't believe what had just happened. Dreamboy and I were in shock, but the homeboys weren't happy that we came back with full clips in our guns. I've always wondered how different things would be if my homeboy's gun hadn't jammed on him. What if the lady and young girl had been caught in the crossfire? Even then I knew I wouldn't have been able to live with myself. And the homies would have disciplined us severely - catching innocent bystanders in the crossfire was a big no-no, especially children. The consequences would have come down hard if that had happened. Not to mention the potential police and legal involvement. I've always regretted my part in it and wish I could apologize to both of them. I have no doubt in my mind that the scene from that day stuck with them, as it has stuck with me.

The homeboy Stranger and I were chilling on 58th Street, in his trailer home that was parked in another homeboy's driveway. He asked me to roll with him to pick up some smokes. It was probably about 3 in the morning. Most of the homeboys had gone home already after a night of chilling on 58th. We hopped in his car and headed to the gas station on the corner of Florence and Compton Ave. We parked next to a gas pump and both of us got out of the car.

Stranger went up to the cashier window on the outside that's used for purchases late at night. He looked back at me and told me to grab the spray can out of the trunk. I was excited at the prospect of striking up on a long, clean white wall. As I was getting ready to, I saw a primered gray Monte Carlo full of bald heads cruising east on Florence Avenue, bumping to the song "Eighteen with a Bullet" by Pete Wingfield. I knew right away it was South Central 18th Street eses, one of our many rivals. Stranger and I both threw up the "F" hand sign and one of their heads popped and screamed out, "SC Eighteenth Street!" I knew we were in trouble because neither of us were packing heat that night.

They busted a U turn and came back our way. Stranger and I took our shirts off, ready to get down, and I hoped to God they weren't packing either. They pulled up and all jumped out of the car. There were a total of six of them, but my homie Stranger said, "Let's go one-on-one, toe-to-toe. If you fools are down for your shit, we'll get down one-on-one. No jumping in." A tall ass, skinny fool called me out. He said, "Was up! Me and you!" So he and I started locking up and we began to exchange blows. It seemed to go on forever. I finally got caught with one dead on the chin. He dazed the fuck out of me and I fell to the ground. My homeboy grabbed me and picked my ass up while I shook it off. Then my homeboy Stranger called out the driver. Stranger beat the fuck out of that fool and dropped him quick. Next thing we know, they all ganged up on us and stomped us out pretty bad. We were both knocked out cold. I woke up to the cops, bruised but happy to be alive. The fools from 18th Street had already taken off by the time the police showed up. They told us the gas station clerk came out with his gun and chased them away before he called 911, so we thanked him for his help. Stranger and I paid a visit to their side of town to follow up after we'd both licked our wounds.

I took many ass whoopings in my hood days. I believe it made me thick-skinned, and rough around the edges. But it also made me paranoid and gave me flashbacks. I constantly look over my shoulder, not because of fear, but because I always want to be ready and don't plan on getting caught off guard. Nights like that turned me into a pretty good street fighter and made me even more fearless than I already was. But it was a hell of a price to pay.

It was after Thanksgiving in 1996 when things were really hot with a rival gang across the tracks. Over a dozen lives were lost, including innocent bystanders, within a year's time. On the night of December 1, 1996, I was in the hood chilling with the homeboys. My pager lit up with "69696969", which was code for a booty call from the girl I was dating at the time. I headed over to the payphone to return the call. Out of nowhere, a van came flying past me accompanied by another vehicle. Within minutes, it sounded like the 4th of July was going down. The snap, crack, and boom of assault rifles was constant for a long time. It seemed endless. I didn't have my heat on me, so there was no way I was going to run towards the gunshots and become a victim myself. I didn't think much about it at first, but I was saved by that booty call. Moving towards the payphone pulled me out of the line of fire.

In the aftermath, we discovered that four lives had been lost. Our rivals had caught the homeboys slipping closer to Compton Avenue. They jumped out of their vehicles and ambushed the homies with assault rifles on the other side of 59th Street. Rest in peace to my homeboys and my deepest condolences to their loved ones. I always seemed to escape death for some reason, just by luck or accident. But death was always nearby, a specter knocking at my door.

The 90's was the business in South Central during the Nike Cortez and crack cocaine era. The LA riots kicked off after the four police officers that beat Rodney King were found not guilty at trial. This verdict outraged the world and led to 6 days of unrest, looting, arson, and rioting centered in the heart of South Central Los Angeles. It all started on Florence Ave, just west of our turf. All hell broke loose - it was absolute madness. Businesses were looted and burned down. Most of the people doing the damage didn't really care about what sparked the violence, but instead just took advantage of the opportunity. And it wasn't like anyone was even trying to hide that they'd been a part of it. If you looked around any trash can, you'd find tons of empty TV boxes, clothes, shoes, you name it. People were literally driving moving trucks right up to grocery stores, liquor stores, and every other type of business and loading up. They took everything they could get their hands on. It was heartbreaking to see South Central LA burned and destroyed right in front of our eyes. It was like watching your home go up in flames and you knew the fire department wasn't coming.

In the summer of 1993, the infamous gang peace treaty was in full effect in Southern California, including South Central Los Angeles. There had been a meeting called by some heavy hitting shot callers at Elysian Park, right next to the Los Angeles Dodgers stadium. All hoods were told to show up there and Florencia was at the meeting representing. The meeting called for all gang violence to cease immediately. There was to be no more war amongst each other - the rivalry and infighting had to stop.

Soon after this meeting, we were invited to a house in the Valley. The fools had metal detectors at the gate before we entered. This was where the toughest fighters from every hood got to go toe-to-toe. It was a chance for enemies to duke it out instead of shoot it out. We also found ourselves playing football with a bunch of different hoods like the South Central Ghetto Boys and B13 gang, and we even invited rivals into our hood to play ball. We went to parties in the 38th Street hood, a longtime rival, something I could have never imagined would happen. Numerous rivals were coming to our hood to party as well. It was an awkward time in the gang world and I'm not surprised it didn't last long. I didn't like it from the get go, but I had to shut up and color. We did what we were told. It was back to business as usual and in no time gang violence was on the rise again.

CHAPTER 14

It was a warm summer day in the hood. I remember it distinctly because I was wearing a wife beater and my homeboys were talking shit about how fucking skinny I was. It was all fun and games, them giving me a hard time like any other day. My homeboy Lil Man was with me as usual. But the day soon took a darker turn.

I had recently broken up with one of the homegirls I had been dating. She was cool people, though. She had a good heart and was very smart. I admired what a good mother she was to her son and how hard she worked. While we were together, she regularly invited me over to her apartment and even taught me how to drive stick shift in her car. But I was a total asshole to her. I was young and naïve. Despite this, she was generous to me in so many ways. She let me use her car even though I didn't have a driver's license. She was in her mid 20's or so, and I was only 15, but I'd lied to her about my age. I told her I was 18 and since I'd always looked older, I don't think she questioned it. One day I was pulled over by the cops for speeding in her car. By the end of the traffic stop, they had impounded the car and let me go. But before they took the car away, I removed the pull-out stereo because I knew if the car was impounded with the stereo still in it, it would be stolen in the tow yard.

I called her to let her know what had happened. She was furious, understandably, and was talking a lot of shit and being completely disrespectful to me. And rightly so - I deserved it. But my temper got the best of me in that moment, so I told her I wasn't going to pay to get the car out of impound and on top of that, I wasn't going to give her stereo back. I was being a little shit. I was selfishly upset and decided to respond the punk ass way. Remember, I was young and dumb and had zero respect for anyone. I was numb to anyone's feelings but my own. It was the absolute wrong thing to do and the worst way to respond to someone I cared about. I regret my part in it and have learned from my mistakes. We stopped seeing each other after all that drama, but it didn't go away.

I would see her around the hood once in a while and we would sometimes say hello. Then I got wind she started talking to one of the homeboys doing 20 plus years in jail and would often go visit him. He had some real juice in the hood, and what he said carried weight. Homies on the street did what he asked, and it was his way or the highway when it came to hood business, even while he was incarcerated. In one of their chats, she told him what went down between us in regards to her car. He wasn't happy about it. There was a phone call that came through to one of the homeboy's safe houses. It was him, this higher echelon homie. He was doing time in the LA county gang module then. He asked to speak to several of the heavy hitting homeboys and then asked to speak to my boy Lil Man. When Lil Man hung up the phone, he came and pulled me aside. He said, "The homeboy wants you out." I asked, "What do you mean he wants me out?" Then Lil Man told me that the homie wanted me jumped out of the hood, which meant they would beat me out. I wouldn't be part of the gang anymore.

He told me because I did his girl wrong and disrespected her, I disrespected him. I was heated, and my blood was boiling. I walked down the street to cool down and came back shortly after. There were two homeboys in the driveway by the safe house where the call had been received. Both were mad dogging me, staring me down with their fists balled up. Ready to jump me. They had clearly gotten wind of what happened. They were two homies I really respected, but never again after that day. I hated feeling shut out, even though I had been in the wrong.

The homeboy in jail called the safe house shortly after and asked to speak with me. He asked me what happened between me and his girl. I explained how it all went down from my perspective. He told me if I wanted to remain a Maldito, I was going to have to take care of some business for him. I said no problem, I got this. He ordered me to find the homeboy Angel, who is now resting in peace, and to confiscate some goods from him. Whatever proceeds came out of that were to be sent directly to him in the Los Angeles County Jail gang module, before he headed to the big house to do some hard time.

I did what I had to do, and I didn't ask any questions. I felt beyond terrible because the homeboy Angel, rest in peace, was actually a solid homeboy. The story was that the homie in jail had asked Angel R.I.P. for a financial favor and Angel gave some push back. So the homie in jail wanted him ousted. That was the word on the street. Now I don't know how much truth there was to that, but it wasn't my place to know or even question it. But let me tell you, I didn't feel good about the situation at all. After the incident with Angel R.I.P., I withdrew from a handful of the homeboys. My circle became smaller than it already was. I felt some type of way. I knew I had betrayed a homeboy who'd always had my back and done right by me. I was a snake in the grass, but I didn't have a choice. My hands had been tied, but I hated cheating my homie.

Angel R.I.P. and I didn't cross paths again for another year or so after this all went down, but I got to set things straight with him before he passed away. He understood that I did what I had to do and knew I was in a tight spot with a homie way more powerful than me. I had a wad of cash in my pocket with a rubber band wrapped around it, and I gave it to him as a peace offering and restitution. There were no hard feelings, thank God, before he passed.

Over the years I heard that my homegirl moved up in the world and made it to the top of the ranks in Florencia. She was very well connected with the upper echelon homies and her word carried weight. She made big news in Florencia and ruffled some feathers as well. She was even known to have "keys to Florencia" at one point, which means that she was the shot caller. May God bless her and her familia, and I wish her the best.

I sound like an idiot when it comes to women based on that story, but it would have been a miracle if I was good at relationships in those early years. I lost my virginity when I was only 10 years old with a girl who was 13. My second partner came around at 13, and she was in her early twenties. My early sexual history was nothing to be proud of, but this was an honest account of me as a young boy: irresponsible, no guidance, dumb, and full of you know what. Most of the girls I dated I treated poorly because I was immature, ignorant, and didn't know how to respect women.

I didn't know what a healthy relationship looked like. Domestic violence filled my childhood and I wasn't around a healthy relationship long enough for it to make an impact. I had zero clue how to treat my girlfriends with dignity and respect. If you were a previous girlfriend of mine, please forgive me because I truly didn't mean it. I'm grateful I've grown as a man and a partner, thanks in no small part to the influence of some truly amazing women.

CHAPTER 15

For gang members tattoos, or tats, can be particularly meaningful, but their main purpose is to advertise your allegiance to the gang. A lot of pride goes into that tattoo, as it shows you're so loyal that you're willing to write it on your body forever. Should you die for the gang, that tattoo is going to the grave with you. And when they're in a highly visible location, it gives any gang rival you meet a big slap in the face and challenges them to defend their gang as soon as they see it.

Gang tattoos send a clear message of membership. Getting blasted with gang ink not only shows a high level of commitment to the gang, but also acts like a receipt after proving yourself. That's why gang members often have their work done in very visible places, like the face, head, neck, and hands. Face tattoos in the 90's were a big thing, not just in Florencia, but in all of the hoods. You had to be hardcore for a face tat. Nowadays it seems like everyone and their momma has a face tattoo. I can only guess they have no idea what we went through in the 90's to earn those. In F13 Malditos, we had our gang tattoos on the sideburns, head, neck, eyelids, ear lobes, you name it.

I got my first tattoos on my side burns when I was eleven. On my right sideburn, I had F13 for Florencia 13 and on the opposite side was MDS for Malditos. That was soon followed by Florencia Trece in cursive writing on the back of my arms. Those tattoos were incredibly painful. They were done by my homeboy with a homemade tattoo gun made out of common household items. This included tools like needle nose pliers, a knife, a Phillips head screwdriver, toothbrush, ballpoint pen, guitar string, a mechanical pencil eraser, an electric motor from a tape recorder, and duct tape. What follows is not an instruction manual on building your own tattoo gun. Do not do this - it's a terrible idea and a real health hazard.

I hung out watching my homeboy build the tattoo machine before he put it to work on me. First, he ripped the motor out of a tape recorder and figured out where the positive and negative wires were located. Then he created a frame for it to sit on from a plastic toothbrush. Once he cut the head off where the bristles were, he melted it with a lighter in order to shape it so the motor rested on it. He took a standard ballpoint pen, emptied it, then pulled a guitar string through the shell. After that, he used duct tape to secure the pen and the motor to the tooth brush. The guitar string acted as the needle and was connected to the motor using the pencil eraser. My homie connected the motor to a power source and fashioned a foot-operated power switch. All that was left was to dip the guitar string needle in ink and he was ready to tat me up.

All my gang tattoos were put on my body at a very young age. The three dots under my eye, Malditos across my chest, F13 block letters on my back, and Florencia Trece on my triceps. The tattoo on my back may have been the most painful. I was twelve when I got it done and it took about four hours from start to finish. We were at my boy Lil Man's baby momma's house that night, just chilling with a bunch of the homeboys and homegirls. I was slouched over the most uncomfortable chair ever for all four of those hours. I had to play the tough guy and stick it out, because I knew I couldn't show weakness. When it was finally complete, I was super proud but more so relieved. My body felt wrung out from the pain and tension of keeping still and quiet. But I also hadn't eaten all day, so I was running on empty in more ways than one.

The homie who did my tattoo grabbed a spray bottle of something, looked back at me, and asked if I was ready. He had a huge grin on his face and I was like, "Ready for what?" He instructed me to turn around and find out. Then he started to liberally spray my back with rubbing alcohol. I wanted to scream so bad, but knew I had to suck it up with so many people around. I almost fainted between the trauma to my body and not eating. The homeboy was laughing so hard that I wanted to give him a one hitter quitter just for that.

I've gotten more tattoos than I can count over the years and I'm still not done. Though the subject matter and my motivation to get them may have changed, the addiction hasn't. Every tattoo has a meaning and a story behind it. A part of my life, indelibly written on my body. I have both of my kids' names tattooed on me and I have some Navy tattoos that I'm extremely proud of. I have Navy chief anchors on my collar and 1893, the year the chiefs were established. Now, tattoo sessions are like therapy for me. I'm just glad I've graduated to a professional artist and upgraded from that homemade gun. While clever, that shit was janky.

I was on the metro rail one day, leaving the hood to go crash out at my mother's house. It was really the only time she saw me. This was after a long night of hustling on the street. I didn't have my heat on me that day, and of course this was when I got caught slipping. On the way to my mom's place, the metro rail made stops in neighborhoods that belonged to F13 rivals. The next hood over was Watts – a long standing rival of Florencia. I sat next to a lady and her grandchild who was probably 5 years old. She was an older woman in her 60's with dark, short hair, and something about her reminded me of my mother. We sparked up a conversation and she asked where I was from, where my parents were born, and if the tattoos on my face hurt. Then she told me she would pray for my safety.

We were coming up on a stop where the eses from Watts were known to hop on and terrorize people. They'd rob them and then get off at the next stop, just like we did at the Florence Avenue station. And sure enough, three fools got on the train. They immediately came over to me and one of the fools asked, "Where you from, ese?" When I responded, "Florencia 13 Malditos," he pulled a strap out of the back of his waistband. It was an all-black 9mm handgun. I stood up in his face, but then he pointed the gun dead at me. My heart dropped. My life flashed before my eyes and I thought this was it. I'm going to die for the hood, right here and right now.

Then I realized I could hear the lady I had been talking to pleading for my life. She said, "No por favor...no lo mates." Please don't kill him. The little girl with her was hugging her tight and I could hear her crying. To make matters worse, he disrespected Florence and said, "I'll kill you right now." I froze. I couldn't move. While I looked him dead in the eye, ready for it to end, everyone else on the train realized what was going on and started to panic. They moved to the other side of the car, trying to get as far away from us as possible.

We were coming up to the next stop when one of his homies snatched the gold chain off of my neck, and grabbed all the cash out of my pocket. It was everything I had hustled in the hood the night before. Then his other homie cracked me right in the chin and shook the fuck out of my brain. I fell back and down to the ground before they got one final kick in to my face. They hopped off the train and I vowed never to go anywhere without a strap again. I know I was a bad person back then, and I'm a big believer that bad things happen to bad people. Karma was always nearby, and karma has no deadline. Maybe this was supposed to be my wake up call, my chance to get my life right, but it wasn't received just yet. I was too focused on the visit I was going to pay those fools.

CHAPTER 16

When I got the tattoos on my face, I was careful to never let my mother see them, because I knew she would have a heart attack. Keep in mind I was only 11 or 12 years old when I started getting inked. Every time I was around my mom, I would be sneaky and wear a beanie on my head. I'd pull it way down past the bottom of my ears so it could perfectly cover my sideburn tattoos. Sometimes I even wore makeup to cover them. I would borrow it from girls I was dating when I couldn't wear a hat to hide them. I knew I couldn't keep them a secret forever, but I was trying to buy as much time as possible.

Early one summer morning, I woke up to someone scratching the side of my face. It was my mom, trying to rub off my tattoos. I had been sleeping soundly on my side, crashed out on her living room floor. She must have gone through every cuss word in the Spanish language, then she started to cry. She asked me to take it off my face immediately. I told her it would never come off because it was a tattoo. That snapped the last thread of her control and she threw her chancla at me. I'm not sure what I was thinking at that moment, but I also decided to show her the huge F13 block letter tattoo that covered a large portion of my back. That's when she told me to get the hell out of her house and I gladly did. I called my homeboy to pick me up and asked if I could stay with him for a bit. He agreed and I started packing. I grabbed my sawed-off shotgun, my handgun that I kept under the couch cushion, and I was ready to go kick rocks for several weeks.

I can only imagine how my mother felt when she saw those tattoos. My son is 13 years old now. I cannot fathom what it would be like to see my young boy with gang tattoos on his face or anywhere else on his body. To say I would lose my mind would be an understatement. I would hunt down whoever did that to my son and have a serious interaction with them. It would break my heart, but it helps me understand how much my mother must have struggled during those years. I'm grateful that he's into video games, social media, and YouTube, and not getting gang tattoos.

How the world has changed. And I'm not sorry that it has. I'm glad he just gets to be a kid. My sister and I never got that chance.

My sister and I used to talk major shit to each other and never saw eye to eye. We didn't move past childish fighting, we just got bigger, stronger, and more angry. If you've ever met Lisa, you know she's no pushover and can throw punches with the best of 'em. Sadly, we both got involved with street gangs at a young age. Lisa was an active member of a smaller gang in the city of Bellflower, called Colonia Flores 13. Her hood nickname was "La Spider".

Even though they were a smaller gang and new to the game, they were active in the streets and held their own. One time, my sister and I were talking shit to each other and she disrespected my gang by saying a degrading name. I went for my gun, pointed it at her head, and told her I would take her life. She was pregnant, and I knew it. The gun wasn't loaded, but that doesn't matter. I still threatened her and her unborn child's life. Just the fact that I could do something so cold-blooded is downright horrific and disgusting. It's hard for me to think of that day, much less talk about it, but I want to clearly illustrate how far gone I was. Lisa wasn't much better. Our teenage, gang-infested minds were so deep in that world that we would do anything for the gang, including threatening and hurting our own flesh and blood.

Lisa was just a teenager when she got pregnant with her first son. When mom realized she was expecting, she threw my sister out. It has been a hard road, but my sis eventually had two more boys and is now mother to my nephews Andrew, Memo, and Carlitos. She's a strong, tough, and spiritual woman who wears her heart on her sleeve. She still possesses the same strength that helped her survive our youth, and she takes no shit from anyone. She has raised her boys on her own and has shown them how not to follow in our footsteps.

Lisa and I now have a great relationship and we can talk openly with one another. It helps to have someone by your side who's walked through the same hell. We look back on our struggles growing up with laughter, chagrin, and occasionally some tears. We didn't know what being loved meant or felt like, and it has hindered us both in so many ways. It's hard for my sister and I to say "I love you" or even to hug each other. We're uncomfortable with simple displays of affection because we never expressed anything like that growing up, and it's just not the norm for us.

But despite the shitty beginning, we're both trudging forward, trying to be better in the second half of our lives than we were in the first. I'm grateful that there are no hard feelings between us. I don't deserve her forgiveness, but I thank God she gave it to me anyway.

CHAPTER 17

One day in 1995, I met a girl in South Central LA on 59th Street. Her best friend was messing around with my best friend and I'm sure you know how the story goes. Eventually, we hooked up too. She had been with a homeboy of mine before me, and I kind of stole her from him. We started dating, and within a few months we were surprised to find out she was pregnant.

My beautiful daughter Emily was born on May 15, 1996 when I was still an active member of Florencia 13 Malditos. Emily was born at Children's Hospital Los Angeles. I want to say a huge thank you to the Children's Hospital and their staff, for what they do every day and for everything they did to save my daughter. Emily was born premature. She weighed in at a mere two pounds and six ounces and was born 12 weeks early. She was placed in an incubator for several months and had a tube down her throat until her lungs fully developed. Every waking moment of those months, I prayed that she would make it and be okay.

She was a fighter even at that age. In my eyes she's a miracle baby who wasn't supposed to be here with us. Now she's all grown up and a very beautiful young lady. I had no idea if she would even make it kindergarten, and now she's in college pursuing an incredible career. But the beginning was touch and go. It seemed like we'd just gotten her home from the hospital when she gave us another scare.

We noticed she wasn't eating well and seemed like she was struggling to breathe. She had a terrible cough. I was scared and drove her back to the Children's Hospital like a man possessed. I think I ran every red light. I was in such a hurry to make it there and get help. They took us to a room so she could be examined, and as soon as the doctor put a stethoscope to her chest, he called for assistance. Before we knew it, she was being rushed to the emergency room for care. She had pneumonia and the doctor was really concerned because her lungs were already weak and compromised from being born prematurely. They treated her for another few weeks in the hospital until she was ready to come home again. She was in bad shape, but Emily was and is a fighter, and even as a newborn had a strong will to live.

For the next two years, I felt like I had two faces. I was living the dad life now, but I was still living the hood life, too. I felt torn, but had no idea how to fix my problem. I'd always wanted a better life for myself, but now I had a family depending on me to deliver on that promise. The pressure built and built until I thought I might burst.

About halfway through 1998, I hit a wall. I was in the hood and it was hot out. I was deep in thought, in an almost meditative state. I was standing on 59th Street trying to double up my paper and make that money, but my mind was far away, reflecting on my life. All I could think was how tired I was of this shit. I'd been running in this drug and gang-infested warzone since I was 11 years old. Most kids that age were at home playing with toys and video games.

Between the cops and our rivals, I was exhausted from constantly watching my back and worrying about how I was going to make a living. I was tired of seeing my homeboys go to jail. I was sick of seeing the homeboys get shot and I was over dodging bullets myself. I was finished being looked at like I was lower than dirt because of my tattoos and how I dressed. I was pissed off by the fact that I couldn't finish regular school because of my gang banging. I felt empty. It had been such a long road.

In that moment, I was keenly aware that my daughter was now 2 years old and had already been through so much. And she was facing the same life I dreamed of escaping. I had turned to the gang because I felt alone and directionless without a father. There was no one to guide me into manhood. No one to support me when life got tough or advise me when I needed to make a difficult decision. While the gang offered me a path, I had found it was destructive instead of productive. I didn't like the person I had become. I was tearing down my community instead of building it and I was ripping my family apart instead of supporting and loving them. There had to be another way.

Emily deserved a better hand than I'd been dealt. And I knew I had it in my power to give it to her. I could offer her more if I could clean up my own life. I owed it to her and to myself to do better, before I ended up dead or in jail for the rest of my life like countless homeboys. And I had burned enough bridges that I knew only a few people on this earth would truly care if any of that happened. Unless I made a drastic move, I was well on my way to complete and utter destruction.

If I had gone to jail right then and done hard time, no one would really have cared but my loved ones. My mom, dad, sister, best friend, and some of my extended family. But that was it. Some will get lucky and have that truly loyal homie that will reach out via letter, take a phone call or two, and maybe even visit. But it's rare. As time passes, you become just a memory, and sometimes not even that. People have their own lives to live and go on without you.

I had seen it one too many times, and could line up countless homies who have done hard time or still are, who will tell you the same thing. A majority of them will say that the homeboys and homegirls have been non-existent while they're in jail. The only ones suffering with them are their loved ones, because that love goes deeper than gang ties. And the truth is, some of the homeboys doing time don't even have family to lean on. I can only imagine what runs through their mind while they're in jail and most if not zero of the homeboys make an effort to reach out. Especially if they're doing time for gang business. The same homeboys that you would take a bullet for in the streets may disappear when those bars close behind you. I know loyal homeboys and homegirls exist and I have mad respect for them, but they're the exception, not the rule.

It was running through my mind in an endless loop. Am I going to jail or am I going to get killed? All because I'm trying to earn respect and stripes for something that gives me nothing in return. Am I going to miss out on the best moments of my life or can I be free to spend precious time with my kids? Can I give them opportunities I didn't have? I knew I wanted to be able to see my loved ones, hug them, watch them smile, and hear their laughter. I wanted to drive a nice car, live in a beautiful home, travel the world, have a rewarding career, and give back to the community I had taken so much from. The ball was in my court and I didn't want to remain on the sideline. I didn't want to miss my shot or just make an easy lay up. I wanted to slam dunk that ball with everything I had. I wanted to start living my life like I was proud of it.

Around this time, I saw a military recruiting commercial on TV. I still remember how it grabbed my attention and how cool it looked. I decided then and there to go see what it was all about and if there was anything in it for me. I didn't tell anyone I was considering the military. I wanted zero distractions and I especially didn't want anyone trying to talk me out of it. If my mind is set on something, I am going to execute it no matter the obstacles. I looked up a local recruiting station in Los Angeles and called several times. No one ever answered the phone, but I decided to make a trip there anyway.

CHAPTER 18

When I got to the recruiting station, I saw there were actually four separate offices. One for each branch of service: Army, Navy, Marine Corps, and Air Force. Keep in mind that at this point in my life, I had no clue about anything related to the military. So, I walked into the U.S. Marine Corps recruiting office first. I rolled up dressed down in my Nike Cortez, oversized Ben Davis pants, a crispy, bright white T-shirt, and my Los Angeles Raiders hat.

There were two Marine recruiters staffing the office that day. One of them approached me and asked how he could help me. He stared me down head to toe and rightfully so. There was a dressed down cholo in his office with tattoos on his face, so I don't blame him. I asked him how I could sign up. He looked at me, smiled, and asked me if I was affiliated with a gang. I smiled back and asked him if it looked like I was affiliated with a gang? We both had a good laugh, but he said, "Seriously man, with visible, gang-related tattoos, no way in hell you have a chance." I sat down with him and explained that I was trying to turn my life around. I had a family I wanted to do right by, but I needed help. The Marine recruiter apologized again, and told me that they had a long-term problem with gang members enlisting. Once they were discharged from the service, they would come home to the hood and use their military training to enhance their street gang. I got what he was saying. I understood and knew I couldn't be upset. The Marine Corps was trying to do what was right and he was just doing his job.

I've always wondered how different my life would be if I had the honor of joining the United States Marine Corps. But the Marine recruiter still did right by me. He suggested I walk next door to the Navy recruiting office, so I thanked him and did just that. I knocked on the door and was welcomed by a young Hispanic Navy recruiter named Petty Officer Lazo. He sat me down and listened to my story. I explained to him that I was looking to improve my life so I could provide for my family in a more positive manner. Then he asked me several questions. "Have you ever been arrested for a felony?" "No." "Have you ever done drugs?" "No." "Do you have a high school diploma?" "Yes." "Are you an American citizen?" "Yes." He seemed pleased with my answers so far, so he asked me to take a mock entrance exam called the Armed Services Vocational Aptitude Battery, or ASVAB for short. I didn't know it yet, but the military loves their acronyms and I was about to learn a ton of them.

The ASVAB is a basic academic test that assesses general science, language, math, and mechanical understanding. A minimum score is required to pass the official ASVAB, and it varies based on the service you want to join. I passed the mock ASVAB, so he had me fill out a bunch of paperwork and asked me to come back a few days later to take the official ASVAB. I went home, but kept where I had been all day a secret. I wanted to keep the news to myself until I had something more concrete to share. But I also didn't want anyone to discourage me, or worse, look at me like I was a failure if the Navy didn't accept me.

A few days later, I showed up to the Military Entrance Processing Station, or MEPS, in Los Angeles to take the official ASVAB. On that day, I happened to be the only one who could watch my daughter, so I brought her along. Don't forget, she was only two years old at the time. Petty Officer Lazo did me a huge favor, and watched Emily for the few hours it took me to finish the test. I felt terrible because I didn't want to leave her with just anyone, but he was staying at MEPS the whole time and was surrounded by other military personnel, so I felt safe. But also, Emily was in her "stranger danger" phase. She wasn't happy being held by people she didn't know. I could see the fear in both of their eyes as I handed her over to Petty Officer Lazo. But he needed to make his recruit quota for the month, and I needed to take that test. Thankfully Emily didn't cry, but when I finally finished and found them, he damn near threw her at me. We were both relieved to have it over. He went above and beyond, and I'm so thankful he kept her safe and entertained.

For me, the ASVAB was difficult. I wasn't a great student in school and hadn't taken a lot of standardized tests. Days later though, the Navy recruiter called me to say that I had passed the ASVAB. The minimum score needed for the Navy at the time was a 31. I passed with a big ol' 34! The low score wasn't great, because it meant I wasn't eligible for many of the incredible job opportunities in the Navy. But I'm a big believer that everything in life happens for a reason, and I know I ended up where I was supposed to be.

Even with my low score, I was excited! It was a blessing in the sky for me. Soon after, it was time to start being in-processed. For the Navy, this consisted of a medical screening, fingerprints, and swearing in. During the medical screening, you had to strip down to your underwear and do a duck walk back and forth across the room for a certain distance. As I was performing the duck walk, the doctor watching me was noting all of my tattoos. I was asked to get dressed and wait to be escorted into another room. In that room sat a Navy chief, with a giant book in front of him. He started asking me what my tattoos were all about, so I told him the same story I told my recruiter. He opened the giant book and I saw it was filled with information about gangs from across the country. The chief paged through until he found F13 in the text.

He told me I'd need a waiver to join the Navy because of my gang-related tattoos. I had no idea what a waiver was, or how difficult it would be to get. The chief directed me to walk next door so I could talk to the commanding officer, or CO, about my tattoo waiver. He instructed me to be respectful and refer to her as "ma'am". I walked into the CO's office and was invited to sit down by the commanding officer of MEPS Los Angeles. To me, she appeared to be a kind, middle-aged woman. She asked me what all this gang stuff was about, and said, "Explain it to me like I'm from the country and don't understand life all that well."

I walked her through my story, the same story I told both the Marine and Navy recruiters about getting off the street. She listened and didn't say much while I talked. But I could see by the look on her face that she didn't really get it. My world was completely foreign to her. So you can imagine my surprise when she said she'd sign my waiver. She put a huge smile on my face with those few words. I'd never had much to smile about, so I distinctly remember how good that one felt. This CO had decided to give me a shot, and she told me not to disappoint her. I gratefully responded, "I won't disappoint you ma'am, that's a promise."

I left MEPS that day feeling good. Better than I had in a long time. I was grateful and felt like my future held real possibility for the first time. The major changes I was facing hadn't soaked in yet, though. I contacted my recruiter, Petty Officer Lazo, and gave him the good news. He was happy for me, and I'm sure he was glad that his hard work and determination had paid off. Shortly after, I was assigned a report date for boot camp. With all those details in writing, I began to tell my family, friends, and my homeboys what I had decided.

The news was met with mixed feelings all around, except from the homeboys in the hood. I could hear the doubt in people's voices when we talked about boot camp. I got the sense that many of them didn't believe I'd make it through. But a lot of my homeboys were genuinely happy for me. Some of them even wished they could sign up, too. Unfortunately, by that point most of them had serious felonies on their record. It's truly a shame because there's no doubt in my mind a majority of the homies would have made great service members, but the streets won. The gang had a stranglehold on them, and they never got a chance to explore a different path.

My best friend Lil Man wasn't happy when I shared my announcement. Neither was my family. My mom didn't think I'd make it. She never said it out loud, but she didn't have to. She was a master of that mom voodoo of making her feelings known without ever saying a word. My sister Lisa wished me luck, but Emily's mom had mixed feelings. She didn't love that I was leaving, but she was supportive of me getting a fresh start. Lil Man later thought about joining the Navy too, but never got serious about it. To this day we wish he could have gone to bootcamp with me. I would have loved to have shared that with my best friend, and the Navy would have gained another amazing sailor. I said my goodbyes to all, and reported to boot camp at Great Lakes Naval Training Station in Illinois on July 9th, 1998.

Now to answer the question I get all too often. How did I get out of the gang? Well, the short answer is that I was one of the lucky ones. I didn't have to face serious consequences. Most members of hard core street gangs can't get out without an extreme beat down. And for some, death is the only way out. Running with the F13 Malditos at such a young age actually gave me an advantage. It was like I was the littlest and youngest brother in a huge family. I was raised by all my big brothers and they wanted to see me do well outside of the hood.

I did my time and put in my work for the Malditos. They respected the fact that I wanted to move on, so I could better myself and provide a life for my daughter that I'd only ever dreamed about. And if they had the same opportunity, many of them would have made the same choice. There was nothing but love and respect when I left. I even rolled up in my uniform once on leave after boot camp and got a great reception. Many of my homies have also moved on from the hood and have done well for themselves and their families. We went from boys to men on those streets, forged out of pain and hardship. None of us is without scars, physical or mental, but thank God we made it out alive.

CHAPTER 19

I was almost 20 years old when I left for boot camp, and I'd never been that far east. I left MEPS with several other future sailors very early that morning. We were rounded up and taken to the airport for the trip to Chicago. I remember feeling nervous but also relieved. It was as if a huge weight had been lifted off my shoulders. The waiting had been torture. I was ready for this new chapter in my life. I had been given a clean slate, and I was excited for what was to come. The chance to finally offer my family a better life was not one I was going to waste. I was tired of running the streets and simply surviving in South Central Los Angeles. But I think it also prepared me for anything that might come my way. I knew I was arriving at Navy boot camp with an advantage because of the hood.

Believe it or not, I was ahead of the game because of my gang life. The Navy needs to train some basic skills into people from all walks of life and backgrounds, and they use boot camp to start that process. It's designed to teach recruits discipline, respect, chain of command, structure, team-work, mental and physical toughness, and how to follow orders and instructions. I already understood what discipline was. In the hood, it was a must. You stay disciplined or you will be disciplined. On the streets you had to earn respect by putting in work and give respect to the homies, especially those in the upper chain of command. We had structure in the gang, rules that everyone knew to follow and every homeboy enforced. Mental and physical toughness were a basic requirement. Any sign of weakness meant you were done. It put everyone at risk. Only the strong survive in South Central. We had to be ready for street war any time, any place. We learned to follow orders, no questions asked from day one.

We were picked up from the airport by a bus and taken to the in-processing building at boot camp. The screaming started as soon as the bus stopped. They were shouting at all of us to get the hell off the bus and get in line inside the building. And man let me tell you, I was getting the business right off the top. I was asked more times than I could count what the hell was on my face? When I told them they were tattoos, all I heard was, "Oh, you think you're a tough guy, huh?" It's not good to stand out right away in boot camp, but there was nothing I could have done about my tattoos.

The hardest part for me was retraining my responses. These Recruit Division Commanders, or RDCs, were getting in my face, screaming at me, and I could do nothing about it. I wanted to punch every single one of them in the mouth. My whole life, if someone got in my face, you better believe I had something to say back. If this had happened on the streets and I did nothing about it, I would be considered no-good, clearly a label no one wanted. This was a struggle for me throughout boot camp, but I stayed disciplined and bit my tongue. I know the RDCs were just doing their job. My daughter helped me get through it all and she didn't even know it. She was my main motivation and the source of my determination. I could feel the fire burning deep down inside, and knew I had to make it to the finish line. Nothing and no one was going to stop me. Because failure and going back to the hood was not an option.

I gained a lot of good training in boot camp. We were taught basic firefighting skills, learned about naval history, Navy rank structure, did a ton of physical training, sharpened our teamwork, and even learned how to march in step. I mastered folding all of my uniform items into little square bits so they could fit in my locker. The RDCs kept us busy morning, noon, and night and I swear we got little to no sleep. I was tired and grumpy every morning. I also got a handful of vaccines, which was probably a good idea, because I don't think I'd ever had one before.

Boot camp was also the first time I saw a dentist. Boy, did he have fun with me. After my initial check up, he had me come back for a follow up, and I left with a whole bunch of metal in my mouth. As if that wasn't bad enough, I got called back again to have all four of my impacted wisdom teeth painfully removed. The soreness lasted for several weeks, but they gave me medicine that had me high as a kite the first several days when the pain was the worst. To top it off, within days of starting physical training, or PT in Navy speak, I hurt my foot. I sucked it up the whole time only to later find out I had a stress fracture in one of the bones on top of my foot. I never told anyone and refused to get medical treatment, because I didn't want my training to get delayed in boot camp. All that being said, I loved basic training.

Upon completion of boot camp, I received my orders to my first duty station with a short stop prior to reporting. I had to attend several weeks of Airman Apprenticeship Training school across the "street" from boot camp. With my low ASVAB score, I didn't have many options for my rate, or job, in the Navy. So I enlisted under the Airman Apprentice program, which is now called the Professional Apprenticeship Career Track, or PACT program. There I learned some basics about aviation operations in preparation for ship life in the Air Department community. After this short school, I was to report to the mighty warship, the USS Nimitz (CVN-68), which was located in Newport News, Virginia at the time.

My first thought was where in the world is Virginia? I knew it was a state but could not have pointed to it on a map. And it wasn't just a culture shock for me, but for my family, too. Emily's mom and I got married right after boot camp, so they joined me in Newport News. Neither one had ever lived outside of California before.

I hopped on a plane to Virginia and was picked up at the airport by the duty driver. He dropped me off right outside the Newport News ship-yard with my sea bag on my back, my duffle bag, and a backpack that between them contained all my uniforms and my entire life. The mighty warship Nimitz was wrapping up a major overhaul before it went back out to sea and returned to the fight.

The duty driver made me feel welcome to my new command and escorted me down to the ship. The Nimitz was berthed way down the pier in a dry dock. It was October, and all I can remember is that I was shocked at the temperature. I had never been so cold in my life. The chilliest night I can remember in California was maybe 40 degrees Fahrenheit. Walking down the long pier to get to the hollowed out ship was painful. I could feel the wind cut right through my gloves, socks, beanie, and jacket. My face felt raw. All I could think was who turned Virginia to the North Pole setting? It had to be 10 degrees with the wind chill.

I had seen aircraft carriers before in pictures, but never up close and in person. As I approached the ship, I was blown away by how small I felt in comparison. With the ship in dry dock, I could see the hull. This thing was massive. I was escorted to the facility afloat that was connected to the ship. It consisted of office spaces and berthings where sailors worked and slept temporarily until the ship was livable again. The Nimitz had been almost completely gutted, I was told, with only temporary lighting up, and no running water or power. I was taken to the Air Department office and was relieved by how warm it was. I dropped my sea bag, and since my chain of command wasn't ready to meet with me yet, I asked the duty driver if he would walk me over to the ship so I could check it out. He agreed. Holy smokes - it felt even more frigid on the ship than it was outside. It was an ice box in there and really dark with just the temporary lights. It had definitely been gutted and there were lots of civilian workers running around. The tour of the ship only lasted about five minutes before I was told to head back down to the Air Department Master Chief's office.

When I returned, there were several other sailors waiting to meet him as well. We were all asked to go inside, where we were introduced to the master chief. He was an older gentleman, but he seemed cool and upbeat. He welcomed all of us to the Air Department and asked us several questions. The last and most important question was what division in the Air Department did we want to be assigned to?

The Air Department consisted of four divisions at the time - V1, V2, V3, and V4 divisions. The whole department was made up of 600-800 sailors overall, and consisted mostly of Aviation Boatswain's Mates, known as the AB community. Each division played a different role in the department during the time-of-flight operations at sea, and while in port. While at sea, Air Department sailors wear different colored jerseys. Each color identifies a specific job. I proudly wear and represent green jerseys all day - I bleed green! During flight operations at sea, with all divisions on deck we look like a bunch of skittles running around.

The rate, or job title, of ABHs were assigned to both V1 and V3 divisions. ABE's were V2, and ABF's V4. We also received undesignated airmen; sailors like myself that didn't join the Navy with a specific job title. When the master chief asked what division everyone checking in wanted to go to, all of the sailors were quick to say V1, V3, or V4. But none of them said V2 and I couldn't understand why. I found out later. Always one to stand out from the crowd, I said V2 and they all laughed at me.

I would be remiss if I didn't give a special shout out to my V2 division shipmates, Aviation Boatswain's Mate (Equipment). I am proud to be an ABE. ABEs are hands down the hardest working sailors in the Navy! I'm not discounting any other rate or the difficulty of their work.

But ABEs are cut from a different cloth and I fit right in. These sailors are engaged in the business of the operation and maintenance of aircraft launch and recovery equipment, catapults and arresting gear, and everything associated therein. They work long hours during flight operations, followed by constant preventive and corrective maintenance so the catapults and arresting gear are ready to go the following day. They work with little to no sleep and very little to eat, often going the whole day with just a frozen box lunch. And they do it all over again, day after day, at sea for months at a time.

There's no holiday routine for V2 division at sea. Everyday was a Monday and a work day, either with flight operations, maintenance, or both. Not to mention being dirty all the time between the lube, grease, and grit involved in operating the equipment and during maintenance. ABEs are an extremely tight knit bunch and are very proud to be part of the AB community. We get the job done, rain or shine, and under any weather conditions. V2 division can be summed up as "the primary mission division, launching freedom, recovering victory" on the flight decks of aircraft carriers. In simple terms, we quickly and safely launched and recovered aircraft on carriers. Through this we supported our ground troops during real world events to include dropping bombs on the enemy – something we called dropping warheads on foreheads.

The master chief agreed to all of our requests and granted our wishes. Division representatives were called to come and get their new sailors. Little did I know that roughly 18 years later, I would be back in that very office. Only this time, I was sitting in the Air Department Master Chief seat, and I was asking all the questions.

CHAPTER 20

I was escorted to the V2 division office and welcomed aboard by the office staff and the leadership. From there, I arrived at my final stop, the arresting gear work center. Arresting gear is the equipment that essentially stops the aircraft on the flight deck during flight operations. Back then, the gear consisted of several huge hydro pneumatic engines, the cables that wrapped around them, and the leads which attached them to the flight deck. I was initially excited. But as I soon found out, all of the arresting gear engines were ripped out so I wasn't able to see them.

I was put to work immediately. After putting my personal belongings down, I threw some coveralls on and grabbed a needle gun and air hoses. Then I was led to a space that was rusted out and ordered to needle gun it, grind it, prime it, and report back to them when I was finished. I remember wondering what the hell I'd signed up for. When I finally took a shower later that day, the stall filled up with dirt, rust, and all kinds of filth that had collected in every nook and cranny of my body. I wasn't a happy camper and questioned for the thousandth time what I'd gotten myself into. I understood much later that preservation of a Navy warship is vital to the material condition readiness of the ship, which in turn maintains the life of the ship. We need our ships to be around for a long time, and if we don't take care of them, they won't take care of us.

The next day at work I asked the leadership when I'd get the opportunity to see the "real" Navy. They told me not to worry, they would be sending me on temporary assigned duty to multiple ships on their way out to sea for training. I was lucky enough to be sent out on several occasions and had the privilege to serve on the USS George Washington, USS Truman, and USS Enterprise. I was grateful for the experience I was gaining with operating and maintaining both catapults and arresting gear. I loved the job. It was exciting, and I already knew I wanted to become a subject matter expert.

I was receiving a lot of praise from my chain of command. I never complained about the long, hard hours of work. I did what I was told, kept to myself, kept my circle small, and just took care of business. Meanwhile, the USS Nimitz was still being worked on in preparation to go back out to sea. During this period, I was eligible for my first leadership promotion to the rank of E-4.

Military ranks are separated between enlisted, noted with an "E" and officer, which uses the letter "O". The enlisted ranks number E-1 through E-9 and the officer ranks go up to O-10. At the top of the enlisted ladder is Master Chief Petty Officer, while Admiral is the highest for the officers. Think of the enlisted side of the military as worker bees and policy enforcers, while the officers write those policies and command ships. E-4 is the first rank in the Navy when you earn the title "Petty Officer". It's also the first rank when you're given more responsibility and expected to lead the E-1 through E-3 sailors. I was excited for the opportunity and ready to lead. This was also my first advancement exam, which would test me on my general military knowledge and ask job-specific questions. I passed with flying colors and was promoted to E-4 my first cycle. It was truly a proud moment for me and I felt a great sense of accomplishment.

While I was attached to the Nimitz, I received orders to go on a seven month deployment aboard the USS Lincoln. Several of us from the Air Department were told to pack our sea bags and get ready to deploy. It was our turn to go out to sea and help their crew, but more importantly, come back qualified. We needed to get the USS Nimitz ready to leave the shipyard and back out for at sea operations. This deployment meant I would have to leave my daughter, something I wasn't mentally ready to do yet. But I knew I was still on the right path. Our lives were headed in a more positive direction, and I felt better about myself as both a man and a father. When the time came, it was extremely hard to say goodbye. I was thankful Emily was still too young to understand, but I hated missing that time with her.

We reported to the USS Lincoln and were ready to take care of business on deployment. I became really close with another sailor that came from the Nimitz to the Lincoln. His name was George, and I took him under my wing and became his mentor. I felt like I had finally turned a corner in my life. I was learning to be a leader and I was making a career for myself. It was a chance to use my experience to help someone else to grow as a sailor and a person. But just when I thought I had escaped the gangs, I got dragged right back into that world.

Within days of checking in to the Lincoln, I was walking on the mess decks, where sailors eat chow. There was a table full of Mexican sailors, and they all looked at me hard. In the hood, we called it mad-dogging. Instantly the gangster came out of me and I said, "What the fuck are you looking at?" One of them got up in my face and asked me where I was from and without thinking, I responded out of pure habit. "South Central Los Angeles Florencia trece! What's up foo'!?" He responded back with, "San Antonio, Texas!" I said, "Was' up?" again and pushed him out of my face. All of his friends got up and then someone jumped in between us and broke it up.

Sadly, that was just the beginning of what was to come. Both my mentee and I had several run-ins with that same clown the whole deployment. It never led to anything other than pushing and shoving, because there wasn't an opportunity to really get down and fight. But damn man, it was annoying and I felt like that kind of shit shouldn't be happening in the military. But I was part of the problem, when I should have been part of the solution. This was proof that you can take the boy out the hood but you can't take the hood out of the homeboy. He tested my gangsta' and it came out. It wasn't a proud moment for me and I didn't like the evidence that I wasn't as far from the streets as I thought. I had a lot more growing left to do. Despite that negativity, I learned a lot on the Lincoln about catapults and arresting gear, I got to see the world a bit, and I even learned how to play chess for the first time.

I never once considered that I would get into the game of chess. I'd always thought it was just a game for geeks. Come to find out, I have an inner geek. There was a Filipino sailor that played chess everyday in the lounge outside of the berthing where we slept. Sometimes I'd just sit there and get a kick out of him annihilating everyone. I didn't understand the game, but it was obvious when he said "checkmate" that he'd won. One day, he asked me if I wanted to sit down and play with him, but I told him I didn't know anything about chess. He broke it down for me, and soon we were playing together regularly. In the beginning, I had no chance. He destroyed me, game after game. But it was so much fun! The game was all about strategy, offense and defense, and thinking moves ahead. If you added a clock, the pressure could be extreme.

Playing chess turned into an escape for me. When I was in the zone, it took me to a different world and helped me get outside of myself. It was like a therapy session. A game of chess was refreshing and such a rush all at the same time. I've always worked well under pressure. The trauma of the streets made me quick on my feet and cool in stressful situations, so the game played to my strengths. It combined hood knowledge with what I was learning in the Navy. Before I knew it, I was giving him a tough game. This was when he showed me how to make things even more intense by playing with a clock. It forced us to think fast and make decisions quickly. When the clock expired, if there wasn't a checkmate, whoever had the most pieces off the board lost. Though I don't play as much as I did on that deployment, I still play for fun. I may never be a chess master, but the strategy I learned from the game has served me well throughout my career.

I'm always amazed at the response I receive whenever it comes up that I play chess. People are quick to judge a book by it's cover, especially when that book looks like a gang banger from South Central. Eses from the hood can play chess, too. Many of the homies learn how to play while incarcerated and I hope it provides them with the same escape from reality it did me. I don't recall his name, but I'm forever grateful to chess and that sailor for strengthening my mental game.

Of all the port visits, the one that stood out to me on this first deployment was Perth, Australia. It lived up to the hype. There were women and families on the pier waiting as we pulled into port. They took a bunch of sailors and welcomed them into their homes. Some of those sailors went AWOL, or absent without leave, and never came back to the ship. Ever. Perth was beautiful, and the people were gorgeous. There was a bit of everything close by - city life, country, low-key bars, dance clubs, and a casino. You name it, Perth had it. I spent most of my time in the casino, because I love to gamble. My buddy and I played black jack, which is a game I normally didn't like to play. If someone else at the table doesn't understand blackjack, their moves can cost you money. Poker is more of my game.

We sat down at a table and the black jack dealer was super friendly. She would actually help us out when we were making the wrong call on our cards. At one point in the game, she shared that the black jack dealer at the next table was her husband. But then, she started to get super flirty and friendly with my buddy. I wondered if she was really married to the dude at the table next to us, and if so, what her plan was for my buddy. We played late into the night. The last thing I remember before I went to the hotel room was that they exchanged phone numbers, and I didn't see my buddy until the next day. Who knows what happened, but I can confirm that stories of port visits in Australia are not exaggerated.

Seven months passed and my first deployment came to an end. It was time to head back to the Nimitz. Our ship was getting ready to be underway and at sea where it belonged. Upon my return to the Nimitz, I discovered we had a leadership change in my work center. I had gotten a few emails from my arresting gear shipmates while deployed to the Lincoln, and they mentioned that this new chief was no joke. My first day back, I met the new arresting gear chief, now retired Master Chief Drew Chinloy. My shipmates had not lied.

I don't remember what it was about, but Chief Chinloy ripped me a new one upon arrival. That was the first true ass chewing I had received in the Navy, and it was a good one. My backside actually felt a bit lighter. But after we had worked together for a while, I began to look up to the chief. He had a presence every time he stepped in a room. He was stern, fearless, and extremely knowledgeable about our equipment and operations. When he spoke, people listened. He took care of his sailors and stuck up for us. I knew he was the chief I wanted to emulate one day.

This was the first time in my Navy career that I knew I wanted to be a chief. Maybe I could inspire and motivate others just like Chief Chinloy had done for me. I wanted to help push them to be a better version of themselves and I was ready to take on the challenge to get there. I started following the chief around and picking his brain. I know I annoyed the hell out of him, but damn I learned so much from that man.

Around this time, I received incredible news. The USS Nimitz was doing a homeport change from Newport News, Virginia to San Diego, California. I was heading home! West coast - best coast. Thanks to the training I received aboard the USS Lincoln, I was qualified to operate the arresting gear controller station during flight operations on the top of the ship. I would be there on the 10th level, working alongside the Mini Boss and Air Boss, as they oversaw all flight operations.

The ship made its way down and around South America, enroute to San Diego, California. The waves were so huge they made their way up on the flight deck. I never thought I would feel seasick on an aircraft carrier, but it was rocking so hard I did. Damn near the whole ship was sick. On one particularly bad day, the ship was pitching really hard due to the state of the weather and the sea. Waves were reaching right to the top of the flight deck. Then I was shocked to learn that we were going to be recovering an aircraft on that same flight deck, full of VIPs from a South American country.

I looked over at the Air Boss and asked him if we were really going to recover an aircraft full of VIPs in these conditions, and he said yes. I set the proper weight for the aircraft on the arresting gear and we were ready to go. The aircraft landed safely on the arresting gear cable, but all of a sudden the aircraft headed to the port side of the ship and though it came to a stop, it was listing off the side. I couldn't believe my eyes. All hell broke loose - a bunch of skittles started running around like crazy. But despite the chaos and confusion on the flight deck, we handled the situation and at the end of the day, no one was hurt, including the VIPs.

CHAPTER 21

We made it home to San Diego, California safely and in one piece. Soon after, I was promoted to E-5, which made me extremely proud. My hard work was paying off, and it was around this time I decided that I loved the Navy, my job, and everything that came with it. I was eligible for reenlistment, so I decided to give the Navy six more years of my life. By the end of that contract, I would have 10 total years of service under my belt. I was honored to have Chief Chinloy administer my oath and act as my re-enlisting officer.

After my reenlistment, it was my turn for a shore rotation, which meant that after four years at sea, I would have three years on shore. With no worries about deploying, this would be a chance for me to recharge and spend time with my family. During my orders window, I was able to select where I wanted to go next. There was a billet, or job opening, available in Monterey, California. I wanted to stay in California so badly. It was an opportunity to be close to my family and friends. Thanks to a stroke of luck, I was selected for those orders. I had never been to Monterey before, so I was excited for my new adventure. It was listed as a general billet, so I had no clue what my job there would entail. I thought even if I showed up and they had me scrubbing toilets, I would absolutely be okay with that.

When I arrived in Monterey, I took a quick tour of the town and I was blown away by how beautiful it really was. The Monterey Bay is picture perfect. What I didn't know was that the Navy command I was reporting to was on an Army base at the Defense Language Institute. I checked into my new command and the first person I met ended up being another one of my mentors, retired Navy Chief Baltazar Hernandez. We were both checking into the command at the same time. After a short conversation, we realized we were in the same business of launching and recovering aircraft on the flight decks of carriers. He was also an ABE by trade, and we looked forward to talking more and working together.

I checked in with the Senior Enlisted Leader, Master Chief Berger (retired), who also became one of my mentors, and he looked through my Navy evaluations to get a sense of where to use me. These evaluations act as our Navy "report cards". He was pleased with my documented performance overall, so he told me I would be assigned to the Navy Military Training division, or NMT. This division was where initial entry sailors, straight from bootcamp, learned how to transition from civilian to sailor in preparation for their rigorous language program. This was their first duty station, so they had no clue what the Navy was about. It was my job in NMT to show them, but at that moment, I had no clue what I was getting myself into.

This Navy community was different, something I had never dealt with or seen before. They were all future linguists and intelligence analysts, so they were extremely smart. Some were too clever for their own good. I found myself having to train them on how to iron their uniforms, shine their shoes, make their racks, clean the threading on their dress shoes, and press and tie their neckerchiefs for their dress uniform. For many, it was the first time they'd been away from home, so I even had to teach basic skills like how to clean and clip their fingernails, do laundry, and clean their barracks room for inspections. It was my job to instill discipline, physically train them, be their life coach, and then finally, to do my main task and teach them general military training. I met a lot of great sailors there, from all walks of life and backgrounds. When I look at promotion lists, I still search for their names. I feel like I contributed to their success and stay in touch with so many of them. My tour of duty in Monterey was three years, and they really flew by.

Several accomplishments stand out to me from that tour that I'm particularly proud of. It was a blessing to be promoted to the rank of E-6 while I was in Monterey. I also completed my Master Training Specialist qualification, which would open up doors for several big opportunities later in my career. I was awarded a Navy Commendation medal as an E-6 during this tour as well. This is an award that is generally reserved for E-7 personnel and above. Hard work, dedication, and the incredible accomplishments of my sailors all made that award possible, and I'm extremely grateful to all who contributed to that. I also took advantage of another opportunity shore duty presented, and started my first online college courses.

Emily loved living in Monterey. I taught her how to ride her bike there and would have her ride down the beach strand while I ran alongside her. She fed all the neighborhood cats and gave each one of them a name. Our neighbors were pretty upset and rightfully so. She fed their cats so well they didn't want to go home. Her mom and I didn't help the situation either. We thought it was cute, so we kept buying the really good cat food so she could keep them hooked. I'm sure they all had to go on diets because of her.

We lived just up the hill from Fisherman's Wharf. The house had a huge patio and deck that overlooked the Monterey Bay. I would often go back there and just relax and reflect on life as I soaked in the calm of the ocean. This tour was completely rewarding and I was lucky to find myself there again in a different capacity. It was years later and at a higher pay grade, but Monterey will always hold a special place in my heart.

CHAPTER 22

After my tour in Monterey, I was back out to sea on another ship. I received orders to the USS Ronald Reagan, and within a month of reporting, I found myself on deployment again. This would be a five year tour for me. It was extremely challenging, because I felt like I was never home those five years. We deployed several times, one of which was an unexpected surge deployment, and we were underway at sea quite a bit between each deployment. Even with the difficulty of being away from home, this was another rewarding tour.

The best thing that happened to me while serving on this ship was the birth of my son, Raul a.k.a. Raulito on September 29th, 2008. He is my mini me and has the biggest heart. I was in the middle of a combat deployment the day he was born. I would have given anything to be there and witness him come into this world, but duty called. Thankfully, I received an email with pictures of him shortly after he was born. I had to do a double take when I saw them, because he was just so beautiful. I remember tearing up a bit and saying out loud that there was no way that beautiful baby boy was mine. I was joking with all of the sailors in my office, who agreed I was way too ugly to make such a gorgeous kid. We all laughed and they congratulated me. I'm glad I at least had people to celebrate his arrival with me, since I couldn't be there in person.

Just a few weeks before Raulito joined this world, I was selected to join the biggest and baddest gang on the planet, the Chief Petty Officers' Mess. I had advanced and would be promoted to E-7, chief petty officer, at just under 10 years into my Navy career. This huge milestone is normally achieved in 14 years or more. This was a profound moment in my life, and the culmination of years of hard work. Aside from my kids coming into this world, this was the best thing that had happened to me. I want to share a little bit about what makes a Navy chief so special.

The chief petty officer, or "the chief", recognized today as the backbone of the United States Navy, was established on April 1st, 1893. With that kind of history comes a great deal of tradition. There are three different chief ranks, starting with chief petty officer at E-7. Informally and unofficially known as "Jefe". It's a slang term that means the person who gives you orders, or the boss. This is followed by senior chief petty officer at E-8, or "senior Jefe", and master chief petty officer at E-9, the "master Jefe".

Chiefs lead our E-6 and below ranked sailors and are charged with enforcing standards and policies, and ensuring good order and discipline. Senior chiefs are expected to lead and mentor chief petty officers, and master chiefs are expected to lead all chiefs. At the end of the day, we all work together and make shit happen.

U.S. Navy chiefs are recognized for their technical expertise within their rating, sharp administrative skills, and strong leadership ability. In the Navy, chiefs act as supervisors, advocates, mentors, leaders, managers, fathers, mothers, sisters, brothers, babysitters, life coaches, and so much more for our sailors. Chiefs are also responsible for training junior officers on how to interact with their sailors and how to do their jobs effectively. Though they outrank chiefs, officers fresh out of the Academy, ROTC, and other commissioning avenues often lack military experience and need a helping hand to learn how to lead outside of the classroom.

In exchange for all of this work and responsibility, chief petty officers enjoy some well-deserved benefits far above anything junior sailors receive. One example is access to the Chief's Mess, known as the "goat locker". A lot of magic happens in the Chief's Mess. We eat, lounge, and shoot the shit there. But it's also where we solve all of our sailors' problems, our Navy's problems, and some of the world's problems while we're at it. It's where we take care of business, and if there is a conflict amongst us, we handle it in the Chief's Mess. We walk out of there one band, one sound.

Being selected and promoted to chief petty officer is a rigorous process, more so than any other enlisted promotion in the Navy. In addition to taking a promotion exam, there's a selection board comprised of senior enlisted and officer personnel that screen your performance record, so they can choose the best and most fully qualified out of thousands of candidates. If you're selected, you still have to survive the initiation process and be accepted by the chief petty officers at your command, before you are accepted into the Chief's Mess worldwide.

Chief petty officers are the true deckplate, or ground-level, leadership of the Navy. They get shit done and make shit happen. More importantly, chiefs personally mentor and guide the professional development of sailors of all ranks. Chiefs wear the same khaki uniforms as officers and are given due respect. Because of all of these factors, the rank of E-7 is unique in the Navy. We are fountains of wisdom and safeguard the technical knowledge that keeps our Navy running. Chiefs are expected to have the answers to everything in Navy life. If we don't personally have the answer, we will use our resources within the Chief's Mess to find it. When sailors are confronted with challenges, they "ask the chief", because they know the chief will have their back and guide them through.

The Chief's Mess gave me that feeling I'd been searching for all those years before in F13. The sense of purpose, family, camaraderie, duty, responsibility, and badass brother and sisterhood I got from being a Navy chief far outpaced anything I experienced on the streets. I had been accepted into a gang that made the Navy and the world a better place. I was involved with a crew that built up the lives of my sailors and improved their career, instead of destroying my community selling drugs and participating in gang warfare. I had finally become a man I could be truly proud of.

CHAPTER 23

Shortly after being promoted to chief, my five year tour on the USS Ronald Reagan came to an end. I received orders once again to Monterey, California for shore duty, but this time I would be in a different role than my first tour there. In Monterey, I was promoted to E-8, or senior chief, with just under 14 years of service. This promotion is normally achieved in 16-20 years.

It was during this tour I had the good fortune to track down the CO from the Los Angeles MEPS that made my career possible. I found her in 2008; she was a retired Captain working at the Naval Postgraduate School right there in Monterey, California. I showed up in my uniform and thanked her for the life-changing opportunity she had given me. I had promised I wouldn't disappoint her, and I wanted her to know I'd kept my end of the bargain. The risk she took on a tattooed gang banger had paid dividends both for me and the Navy.

It was a great tour for me once again professionally, but in my personal life, I was hanging on by a thread. This would be the last time that both of my children lived with me. They moved back to Los Angeles with their mother, as we found ourselves facing irreconcilable differences. This was one of the most difficult times in my life, and I was in a dark place because of it. I had become a better version of myself, a stand-out sailor, and finally a Navy chief. All of that came before being a good husband. But I was determined to weather the storm and eventually see the sunlight again. I knew I needed a paradigm shift, a distraction, something new to ease my mind. So, I took up running like never before in my life. Running became my therapy. I learned how to run for fun, run to clear my mind, and to run from my problems and my empty house.

I discovered that running refreshed my mind, body, and soul. I could put my favorite music on in my headphones, leave this world, and go somewhere else. Running was my life saver. It helped me get through the days of misery, knowing my kids weren't with me any longer. Over the years, I started to run further and longer. In 2011, I ran my first half marathon in Big Sur, California and finished in 1 hour and 51 minutes. After that, I ran the 15k Hot Chocolate in Seattle, Washington. It's a shorter distance but, in my opinion, was more difficult since the route included several hills, one of which was more than a mile long, and I ran the whole race in the rain. I sprinkled in several smaller races over the years, but in 2019, I decided I wanted to run my first marathon.

I'll be the first to admit, I didn't train as I should have, but I'd already made up my mind to do it, so I was committed. About a week before the race, I ran the furthest distance I'd ever run in my life - 20 miles. I figured if I could run 20 miles, what was 6.2 more? I had already signed up for the Rock 'n' Roll Marathon in San Diego, California and there was no turning back. Even a knee injury just before the race wasn't going to stop me. The morning of the race I was nervous. I hadn't slept much at all the night before. Probably pre-race jitters. But running through the streets of San Diego was a blast. There was a ton of support from local residents and sponsors, with drinks, shots, beer, and memorials all along the race route. Even with all of the cheering, I hit a wall around the 21 mile mark.

I was running down a hill and felt excruciating pain in my injured knee. After this downhill stretch was more than a mile of solid, uphill climb. I thought there was no way I could finish the race between my knee and that hill. But I was wearing my "Navy Pride" shirt that day, specifically a Navy chief shirt. And in that moment when I wanted to give up, an angel from heaven ran up beside me. I didn't know she answered to "ma'am" and was a Navy lieutenant yet, but as she came up along my left side, she asked, "What are you?" I looked over at her, confused, and repeated, "What am I?" She said, "Yes, chief, senior chief, or master chief?" Understanding dawned, and I said, "Ah yes, master chief." She said, "Good, I know you can motivate me up this hill. I need some motivation."

She had no idea my knee was injured and that the pain had almost become unbearable. She didn't realize that I wasn't just going to motivate her up the hill, but that she was what I needed to push me up it, too. We both hyped each other up as we pushed hard to the top. Words of encouragement came from both sides, and before I knew it we had crested the hill together. Once we made it to the top, it's like I saw red. Even though my knee pain was steady, I put the afterburners on. In my mind, I imagined that my children and my friends and family were all at the finish line waiting for me. Cheering me on, even though I knew it wasn't the case. This mental picture gave me the fuel and fire I needed to finish the last several miles, and make it to downtown San Diego.

Once I turned a corner and could see the finish line, I was euphoric. I had goosebumps all over my body and couldn't believe the rush of energy I got to finish. I gave that final stretch all I had and came in strong! I'm proud to say I completed my 26.2 mile run in under 5 hours. I witnessed that our bodies could be pushed past the limits we place on ourselves. For me, it took teamwork, determination, the will to succeed, a fire burning within me to finish, mental and physical toughness, and a lot of heart. When the pain came, I did my best to compartmentalize it – if you don't mind, it don't matter. I wasn't born with this outlook, though. I had to condition myself to respond that way, and the Navy helped train me to do it. It's why I believe anyone can, because I've seen the transformation in so many sailors. The hardest part is getting off the couch and getting started. If you want it, go out and get it. This philosophy applies to everything, not just marathons. If you push yourself, you'll be surprised what you can accomplish.

Around this time, I was also honored to attend and graduate from the United States Navy Senior Enlisted Academy located in Newport, Rhode Island. This is a leadership development program for active duty senior enlisted personnel E-7 - E-9 from all branches of service, as well as international service members. The Senior Enlisted Academy facilitates courses on leadership, management, national security, and physical readiness. If I thought it was cold in the state of Virginia, I learned that Virginia has nothing on Newport, Rhode Island.

When I arrived at the school, I met Rob Alviso, USMC, who I ended up serving with later onboard the USS Nimitz during our combat deployment in 2017. He asked me if I wanted to go for a run on base and I agreed. It was freezing cold outside and I could feel the icy effect of the water nearby as it sent chills down my spine. The temperature was a balmy 10 degrees that day, but with the wind chill it was around 0 degrees. I put on my Navy-issued PT gear, which consisted of Navy sweats and a Navy sweater. I added a beanie and some gloves. We met outside of the school building ready to get going. Our run started out at an easy pace, warming up side by side. The cold air filled my lungs and the wind cut right through my clothing. It had snowed recently, and there were still several inches of accumulation all around us. By the time we were 30 minutes into the run, I was more than ready to head back to the warmth of my room. My Marine brother was a trooper. I looked over at him and he looked as if the run hadn't even started to faze him. Finally after 45 minutes in, we started to head back.

When we returned to the building where my room was, I noticed it felt like my body was on fire! I'd never had this weird, post-workout-in-freezing-weather sensation before. I ran up the stairs and stripped off my sweaty, yet stiff from the cold, clothing. I noticed that my body was bright red from my neck down to my knees and thought, what in the world? I hopped into the shower in a panic and turned the water to as hot as it would go. The pain intensified. It hit me like a ton of bricks and I almost passed out. My body felt like gasoline had been poured on it. The fire I felt on my skin when I first returned had been ratcheted up by the hot water. I jumped out of the shower and just laid on the bed. My body was simultaneously an inferno and also super numb. I panicked for a moment and decided to turn the water on warm and just relax. It worked, and slowly but surely, before I knew it, I was okay and back to normal. Yes, I know I'm a dumbass and should have known better. Even worse, I should have thought about the basic first aid training I've received throughout my career. Consider this my cautionary tale and maybe your first cold weather run will go better than mine.

Our class started the following day. I was a bit nervous because I knew the academic portion of this course would be extremely challenging for me. The description of the program made it clear there was going to be a lot of required college-level research and writing. Sure enough, within three days, I was completely overwhelmed academically and thought to myself that there was no way I could make it through. I had to take a break, look in the mirror, and compose myself. I needed the reminder that there's no quit in me, and that I could and would succeed.

I have no doubt that a positive attitude, hard work, and determination got me through that demanding course. Once I recentered myself and refocused on my motivation, there was no stopping me. My drive for everything I do in life is my two kids. They don't know it or really understand, but they push me to and past my own limits like no one can. I want to succeed for them, to one day make them proud of me. And I want to seize every opportunity I have to make myself a better person. If I'm lucky, I'll also be able to pass that hard-won lesson on to them.

I put in a lot of extra hours, more than most of the students. Everyone else gave off the impression that they were well-educated, so it seemed like a breeze to them. While most were out enjoying their evenings in town after class, I was burning the midnight oil researching, writing, and preparing for my speeches and tests. I am proud that my hard work paid off and I graduated from the course. But more importantly, I am grateful I had the opportunity to attend. I learned so much, and proved to myself that I could hang in there academically. I highly recommend the Senior Enlisted Academy to all senior enlisted leaders of every branch of service and to our allies. Hands down the best course I've been through in my entire 23 years of military service.

After I completed the Senior Enlisted Academy, I started a new tour in Virginia on the USS Ford, the newest aircraft carrier in the Navy at the time. With a new carrier comes new technology, so I was recruited to assist with standing up the state-of-the-art catapult and arresting gear systems. It was a challenging tour professionally and I had the honor to work with some great shipmates. On the personal front, I'm thankful it was a short tour.

I was miserable in Virginia for so many reasons, but mainly because I was 3,000 miles away from my kids when they needed me most. Few people knew that I was in a really dark place, because I never reached out for help. Instead, I tried to drown my demons so I didn't have to face them. But drinking couldn't erase the fact that I was separated from my family and friends, and I had no support system. I was also in a long-distance relationship, and it hurt me to be apart from her. I wasn't a fan of the weather or the three-hour time difference with the west coast. And worst of all, I couldn't find a decent taco to save my life. It was a huge military town and many of the civilians I met were not fans of the military, owing to the fact that most of the criminal activity in the area was committed by service members. I don't blame them.

The darkness only hit me when I got home. I lived alone and it made me acutely aware of just how lonely I was. Running was my savior, but I also met two people who brought so much light to that dark time. Chris and Bri filled my life in Virginia with friendship and support. They welcomed me into their home and made me a part of their lives. Chris would hang out at my place where we would have deep conversations or just talk about and watch sports. Chris is such a sports fanatic that he could be a commentator on ESPN Sports. He's that good! Bri was always so sweet to me, and together they showed me I wasn't alone and kept me sane. They were meant for each other and eventually got married. I was honored to be invited to their wedding in South Carolina and to act as one of the groomsmen, something I had never done before. I'm grateful this pair dropped into my life just when I needed them most.

Another unexpected path out of the darkness for me in this rough patch was church. I'd never been the religious type, read the Bible, or really even gone to church. But I always believed in the man above, in God. I never doubted that God watched over my life and sent down guardian angels to save me on many occasions. He has clearly had a path for me, and I pray I will continue to walk it.

There was a church in the local community that I started attending after I found it online. It gave me another reason to leave my apartment and grew my local support system. On one particular day, I felt as if the pastor was speaking directly to me. As if he knew all the thoughts running through my mind and could see right through the front I put up. I felt an overwhelming presence wash over me. And then it happened. All the hurt, the hard times, the struggle, the hate, the ugly parts of my life broke free and came flooding down my face. I broke down. I cried like I never had before. All the bottled up emotions, trauma, and pain I had collected for so many years just came rushing out.

Then all I felt was relief. A sense of calmness and peace. And instead of feeling shame or like I was less of a man, as I'd been taught to feel, I felt strong. I was free of this huge, old burden that weighed me down. A sweet lady came over and asked me if I was okay and even patted me on the back. Before that day, I couldn't remember the last time I had truly cried. Or even just processed what had happened to me. I've always compartmental-ized my emotions and certainly would never dare to do something like that when I was running the streets. I walked out of the church that day feeling lighter than I had in years. I know it takes more than one good cry to deal with years of turmoil, but I felt like I had the fresh start I needed.

I was slated to serve a five year tour on the USS Ford. It was going to be a long road. I communicated to my chain of command my desire to get back to the west coast. By some stroke of luck, I knew someone who knew someone that totally looked out for me. I'm certain they didn't realize how much that meant to me and how it changed my life for the better. There was an opportunity on my old friend, the USS Nimitz, to be sta-tioned in the Pacific Northwest. It wasn't California, but I was at least back on the same coast and in the same time zone as my family.

CHAPTER 24

In 2015, I decided to use laser removal to get rid of the tattoos on my face, specifically the three dots under my eye and both of my sideburn tattoos. This decision was motivated by several things. The main one was the danger they put those around me in, including my family and friends, if an old rival confronted me. I can't tell you how many times my tattoos got me into fights. I have been a target at grocery stores, in the streets, and on the beach, and it has even escalated to guns being pointed in my face. Also, I was a professional in the United States Navy and I wanted my appearance to reflect that. And I was growing increasingly tired of being asked what the tattoos on my face were all about. Those interactions made me feel uncomfortable, because I didn't like being stared at and I was over feeling judged.

The laser removal process hurt more than getting the actual tattoo itself. The ones on my sideburns took several sessions to remove because they were so deep in my skin. Want to know what a removal session feels like? You know when you're cooking with grease and it snaps, crackles, and pops as it hits your skin and burns the hell out of you? Well, that's how it felt on my face. As if hot grease was being splattered all over it. I could literally smell my flesh burning. I highly recommend it to anyone who wants to get rid of some old ink though. I got the results I wanted and the pain was totally worth it. And now I feel like my tattoos reflect more of who I am a person, not the boy I once was.

My face tattoos weren't the only baggage I had left over from the streets. I've touched on some of the girlfriends I had in my younger days, before I was with my wife for 17 years. And I've had many important relationships after my marriage. Through these I've learned a lot about myself. I've learned what works for me and what doesn't. While I know there's always more to learn, I now understand the importance of a solid foundation in a relationship, and how to build on that and grow from there. I am by no means perfect, but as someone who has learned so many lessons the hard way, I thought I'd share some insight I've gained.

We all make mistakes or poor choices, but they're any opportunity to grow if you let them be. Every serious relationship has made me a better person overall. But starting from a place of trauma, abuse, and violence meant that I was far behind the curve in emotional intelligence. I drove some good women out of my life, and hopefully I can help someone avoid some of the same traps I fell into. To protect the privacy of the people who have meant a great deal to me, I am going to focus on lessons I learned more than on the women themselves.

My first real love came into my life in Las Vegas, Nevada. I was sitting at the bar having a drink, when I looked over and locked eyes with her. We exchanged a brief smile. We took the next step, talked, and believe it or not a serious relationship grew out of that one little encounter. She was my first love, and I didn't meet her until my mid 30's. She was the best thing that happened to me, and she entered my life as I was struggling with the transition out of my 17 year relationship. She showed me what true love was. Her sweetness, kind heart, and genuine spirit just bowled me over.

We were in a long-distance relationship and had plans to spend the rest of our lives together. Everything seemed so perfect; she was perfect. But the demons from a previous relationship started to come to the surface and I slowly but surely started to push her away. I lost her after several years, and was extremely heart broken. It's clear to me now that I went into that relationship broken and hurting, and instead of addressing my pain and baggage, I brought them along for a free ride into something new. If I had worked on myself more before I met her, maybe I could have saved us both some heart ache.

When I was stationed in the Pacific Northwest, I met an ex-NFL cheerleader for the Seattle Seahawks, a "Sea Gal." She was fun, tall, wicked smart, blonde, and very curvy. To me, she was totally out of my league. I never wrapped my head around how she could fall in love with me. I think she liked the contrast between thug and gentleman in me, but I could be wrong. Maybe I represented something novel and a little bit dangerous. But at the same time she knew she was safe. I was heartbroken when she eventually moved on to another man.

Chemistry, passion, and trying something new are exciting, but there has to be substance and a real connection to make a relationship work long term. Enjoy those fun detours with someone you may think is out of your league, or who is completely different from you. Maybe you'll discover new food you love, an incredible city you would never have visited, or an unfamiliar band while you're outside of your comfort zone with them. But without values, interests, or goals in common, know you're just tourists in each other's lives for a season. Take the lessons you learn and wish each other well when you move on.

I fell hard and fast for another woman while I was stationed in the Pacific Northwest. She had an awesome cat who became my buddy. Several months after meeting and falling for each other, I was set to leave for a deployment. She hated that I had to leave, and the goodbye was heartbreaking. But she showed me the difference communication can make while I was deployed. I received an email from her everyday and even a package or two while I was at sea. That meant the world to me, because I'd never had that before. I felt truly cared for. The longer deployment drug on though, the more opportunity my demons had to rise. I was foolishly letting my past insecurities take over me and I pushed her away as well. When I returned from deployment, we saw each other briefly. But it was too late. I had burned that bridge, and the trust was lost for good.

Prior to my deployment, she wanted me to meet her parents. It was a huge deal for her, which made it a huge deal for me. She was so excited, but also incredibly nervous. The plan was to meet at a restaurant and have lunch. I arrived with a bouquet of flowers for her mom, and I'll never, ever forget the look on her mother's face when I approached the table. I handed her the flowers, and said hello. She gave me the evilest evil eye I have ever witnessed in my entire life. I wouldn't wish that evil eye on my worst enemy in the hood. Her father was rather calm and said hello.

We sat down and I could see that my love was still extremely nervous, but her mood was quickly morphing into sad and upset. Her mom didn't say a word and didn't eat anything. She kept eyeing me. I was so offended, angry, and beyond myself that I started shaking. I'd never felt so disrespected, belittled, ridiculed, or judged like that before in my life. I felt even worse for my love. She could see that her mom had found me unworthy at first sight. I bit my tongue and kept my cool, but only because I didn't want to cause my love any more stress.

I share this story not because I want you to feel bad for either of us, but to point out that a relationship is never just two people. At some point, you will have to deal with your significant other's whole circle of influence. And that can be tricky to navigate, especially if you come from two entirely different backgrounds. After our lunch, I learned that her mother didn't like the fact that I was a cholo and didn't feel I was good enough for her. I respect that and understand that moms want the best for their child. What I don't respect is that her mom didn't even give me a chance to show her who I was under the cholo exterior. I have no lingering hard feelings towards her, and I hope God can put peace, love, and harmony in her heart.

This incident motivated me to let go of another thing I'd held onto from my hood days. Even though I had left gang life behind for the military, I still dressed and looked a bit thuggish. My hair was still buzzed, I wore baggy pants, and had a mustache. You get the picture. For the first time, I decided to grow my hair to a nice length and style, and even changed up my wardrobe. What started as a painful encounter actually gave me a fresh start and was a turning point in my life. I decided to put more effort into showing the world the man I'd become instead of the boy I once was.

The main lessons I've learned from all of the incredible women who have crossed my path may help you make fewer mistakes than I have. Be intimate, and often. And I don't just mean in the bedroom. Get to know each other's hearts and work to keep that closeness a priority despite busy lives. Work on your communication and if you think you're talking enough, do it more. Then increase that. Lift each other up any chance you get. Cheer your partner on and support their dreams. When things get tough, be patient and understanding.

Be completely honest, even when it's difficult and when you think it'll make you look bad. Vulnerability is a strength, not a weakness. Forgive mistakes fast and completely. Let go of bitterness. Want your partner to win, and help them succeed. Make your relationship your highest priority. Learn each other's love language and shower each other with it daily. Trust is the cornerstone of the whole deal - if you can't learn to trust each other, save yourselves the heart aches and move on. Don't live in the past. We all have baggage and past demons to work through, so if they start interfering, try to be patient and understanding. Talk through it calmly and give them time to heal. Love and pour your heart out to one another like it's your last day together. Tomorrow is never promised.

At the end of the day, we all deserve to be treated with dignity and respect and to find happiness in a relationship. Life is too short to be miserable at home. I've learned that trust and healthy communication is absolutely crucial in a relationship. When in doubt, make more deposits than withdrawals from the love bank.

CHAPTER 25

Let's rewind to the master chief that checked me into the Air Department in Virginia when I first joined the Navy. Well 18 years later, I was about to fill his shoes. The USS Nimitz had a new Air Department Master Chief and I was super excited to be closer to my kids and back on the west coast. Washington state was a beautiful place. I lived in Seattle and loved the city, especially riding the ferry to work and back.

I was promoted to master chief or E-9 onboard the USS Nimitz. As the highest enlisted rank in the United States Navy, it normally takes 20 plus years to achieve this honor, but I managed to add that second star above my anchors in just under 18 years of service. I love how everything came full-circle for me. I reported to this ship as an E-1 in 1998 and 18 years later I was promoted to master chief in the same place. The feeling of being promoted to E-9 was indescribable. I was blown away and extremely flattered. Master chief petty officers make up a whopping 1 percent of the US Navy, which has more than 340,000 personnel. I'm extremely proud to be one, walking alongside the heavy hitters and masters of their craft in the world's finest Navy.

I worked hard to make sure my selection to master chief didn't change my character. Authority and influence are sneaky, and can corrupt even the least power hungry person. It's a common pitfall when people make it to the top of any organization. My aim was to focus on the extra trust placed in me and the additional responsibility on my shoulders. I vowed to turn the volume up to full blast and pay it forward to my sailors, subordinates, and our Navy.

Being selected to master chief meant no longer worrying about my career. It was about building my sailors to be winners! I wanted every sailor I came in contact with to be afforded incredible opportunities, like those that had helped me succeed. I did this through direct mentorship, positive influence on evaluations, awards, ranking boards, sailor recognition boards, training sessions, and by providing sound advice to my junior and senior officers alike. My job was to pay my blessing forward, and I will continue to do so as long as I serve.

The rank also comes with its fair share of problems. The two stars above that anchor can be heavy when we take on all of the responsibility for the problems our sailors face. The only way to overcome it is by leaning on our fellow master chiefs and our own mentors. Even with their support, it can be lonely at the top. Sometimes the people we're trying to help forget that we're human as well. And with that extra responsibility for others, we tend to take less care of ourselves. We may tirelessly advocate for our sailors, but that leaves our own tanks empty.

While serving on the Nimitz, I was selected to be a member of the Navy's E-8 selection board in Millington, Tennessee. This board was composed of senior enlisted personnel and officers from various commands who were charged with choosing the most qualified chiefs in the Navy for promotion to senior chief. We screened thousands of records and selected the very best and brightest for promotion to the next higher pay grade. Unfortunately, the Navy uses a quota system, so there are only a certain number of slots available and not everyone eligible for promotion can be selected. Competition was stiff, but I'm confident our team selected the cream of the crop for their well-earned promotion. An unexpected bonus of that opportunity was that I can now prepare future chiefs, senior chiefs, and master chiefs for promotion based on my experience with the selection board.

I want to share a negative experience I had onboard the USS Nimitz during that second tour. My primary duty was as the Air Department Master Chief, leading and managing around 30 chiefs and senior chiefs, 600-700 sailors, and providing counsel to 10 officers. We were all engaged in the business of launching and recovering aircraft on the flight deck during flight operations. Of those chiefs and senior chiefs, I was lucky that overall, they were a solid, hard-working bunch. They took care of chief business on a daily basis and made my job easy. Sadly, there was one chief that was malicious and determined to inflict harm on our department because he didn't get his way.

When I first reported to the USS Nimitz, this particular chief was fired from his primary job due to leadership and management shortfalls within his area of responsibility. He was transferred to work with the Air Department team and the previous department master chief. Shortly after being promoted, I took the helm of the Air Department. We were getting ready to go on deployment, and this chief was coming up on his time to depart the Navy and retire. He submitted his request, but "Big Navy" rejected it. Our Navy needed this chief to deploy for one last ride before he retired. Now let me interject and say that I understand how frustrating it can be when the Navy's plans and your own are at odds. I have had it happen to me more times than I can count. We all take some time to express our irritation and resentment, but at the end of the day, most of us get our attitudes right, put our heads down, and get the job done. It's what we signed up for, even when it's not fair.

This chief was very upset about the decision and understandably so. I afforded him every opportunity possible to spend time with his spouse prior to deployment. I would often let him leave early in the day just for that purpose. At the time, he was in charge of an important program, and he started to neglect it. It was a program that affected our sailors' careers and well-being, so I couldn't let that slide. He had been in his own office, but when he started dropping the ball I moved him to mine so I could keep tabs on him. The next thing I knew, he was hanging outside in the passage-way, or hallway, ensuring everyone who walked by knew he didn't have an office or a computer to work on. It didn't matter that it wasn't true, he just wanted to make waves and make everyone else as unhappy as he was.

By the time we deployed, things got much worse. He accused me, along with several of the Air Department chiefs, of disturbing his rack, or bed, breaking his laptop, cutting holes in his work uniforms, and of drawing pictures with obscene gestures on his spouse's picture. He went on to say that we cornered him in the berthing area and bullied him. None of this was true. During this time, I was personally inviting him to eat chow with us and even participate in group work outs. He agreed to both on many occasions.

I would never allow such awful behavior under my watch. I am confident that the other chiefs I worked with would never stand for it either. I have never tolerated bullies or hazing, and my mission since I picked up my first leadership position in the Navy has been to support, uplift, and give everyone under me the tools they need to succeed. Generally, I don't like to assign motives or see the worst in people, but this situation went way too far for me to give this guy leniency or the benefit of the doubt.

I knew what the chief's agenda was. He didn't get his way to retire as he requested, and he didn't want to deploy. When he was forced to go anyway, he figured out a way to get off the ship. He filed a formal complaint against me and a few of my chiefs for bullying and hazing him. We were pulled into an office and read our rights before being questioned. I was furious. And I was embarrassed. I asked the investigating officer if it was a joke. I told him if any of the allegations were proved to be true, he could have my anchors. I was happy to vouch for my whole department. None of what we had been accused of had ever happened.

The whole ship was talking about it and comments were made even in the Chief's Mess. "Ooohhhh, here come the Air Department bullies." I was getting calls from shipmates from across the country. It was a super frustrating situation, and I felt 10 times worse for the chiefs that were accused with me. This chief eventually got what he wanted, and was flown off the ship during the middle of a combat deployment.

When the investigation was complete, his claims came back unsubstantiated. There was no shred of evidence that anything this chief had accused us of was true. But the fallout continued, despite the results of the inquiry. There was a stain on all of our records. I had applied to the Command Master Chief, or CMC, program and the personal qualification standard, or PQS, program before all of this ugliness went down. Afterwards, my requests were pulled, and I was no longer being considered for either. The CMC program was a special course that only master chiefs could apply for and only elite master chiefs were selected. I felt like I had a great shot to be accepted, and I hated that my dream got squashed that way. I'd rather lose because I didn't meet a standard or because there were better applicants than me. When I made master chief, I was determined to perform well enough to apply for the CMC program. And after all that mess, I never applied again. I have, however, volunteered to fill the role of acting Command Master Chief at two separate commands, including once while at sea during the COVID pandemic.

I'm a big believer that everything in life happens for a reason and that the man above has a path for us. As disappointed as I still am about the situation during that deployment, I've come to accept that the CMC program wasn't on my path. So, I've stayed the course in the AB community, and I've never looked back.

Following this tour, I reported to the USS Makin Island for a four year stint in San Diego, California. This was my first tour on an amphibious assault ship, and I was privileged to serve alongside our brothers and sisters in arms in the United States Marine Corps. I couldn't have been more excited about being back in my home state and closer to my kids, friends, and family. This tour was a hell of a ride to say the least, because none of us foresaw the COVID-19 pandemic.

This was a challenging and rewarding tour for me and the sailors under my watch. There were a lot of wins for the Air Department, where I once again served as the Air Department Master Chief. The transition from aviation Navy, or the aircraft carrier world, to surface Navy on an amphibious assault ship was one of the many challenges. Daily operations on an aircraft carrier are set. They are routine and take place like clockwork. All we had to do was maintain those operations and stay the course. Surface Navy felt like we were always re-inventing the wheel, everything happened last minute, and a lot of the policies, rules, and regulations didn't make sense to me. I don't believe in complaining without being part of the solution, so I let my voice be heard and did my part to make a positive difference.

When I arrived on the Makin Island, I was pleased to find I had a solid group of chiefs, sailors, and officers that supported me. I had the pleasure of working side by side with two seperate Air Bosses, Captain Testa and Captain Emerson, two reliable men and naval leaders that were all about the mission and the sailors. I'm confident we were a dependable team and I advised them on all enlisted sailor matters to the best of my ability.

During my tenure, I loved to say "We stay winning in the Air Department!" There were countless promotions at all rank levels, including meritorious advancements, awards, high command level evaluation rankings, and countless accomplishments involving safe and efficient flight operations during training cycles and deployments. One proud accomplishment that stands out to me is that of Aviation Boatswain's Mate Chief Stephanie Peterson. She initially served as my Air Department Leading Petty Officer. She was an underdog, so her appointment was an unpopular choice. But I saw a lot of potential in her. She became my mentee and I kept my foot on her neck. Not physically of course, but metaphorically. I pushed her to be a solid leader, sailor, and person, and passed on the tools I had been given to advance my career. She rose to every challenge set before her.

So much so that after one year, she was selected as Makin Island's Sailor of the Year from more than 100 First Class Petty Officers. She was also named Pacific Fleet Aviation Boatswain's Mate of the Year. This is a big deal in the AB community, as they pick one sailor each from Pacific Fleet and Atlantic Fleet per year. She was only the second female selected since 1976. She won for the west coast out of all E-6 AB candidates from all ships and shore duty stations. That was a big win for our department and our ship as a whole. The bigger prize was delivered soon after when she was selected for chief petty officer. It was the icing on the cake and I was extremely proud of her and our Air Department team.

My tour started off with the USS Makin Island in a shipyard period to outfit the ship with the latest warfighting capabilities and to be able to operate with F-35 Joint Strike Fighter aircraft in the near future. Once the shipyard period was complete, it was time for the training cycle leading up to deployment. Another challenge was changing the mindset of our sailors from a shipyard mentality to a warfighting mentality. Boy, let me tell you that was like pulling teeth. But the leaders of Makin Island came together and made it happen. Before we knew it, deployment was at our doorstep. Then COVID hit the world and all hell broke loose. Months before we were able to test for COVID, more than 20 sailors, including me, were all sick with flu-like symptoms during an at sea period. We were quarantined in a large medical ward room on the ship.

I'll never forget the feeling. For me, it started on a Thursday night, the day before we were supposed to go to sea. My throat was a bit scratchy. The next morning, I walked on the ship, put my personal belongings away, and headed towards my office. Within half an hour of sitting at my desk, reading and replying to emails, I felt extremely weak and faint. I could barely move. I remember I was asked if I was okay, and I replied, "Hell no." I sucked it up for another few hours, when I noticed I felt really hot. I informed my chain of command that I was going to lay down in my rack for a bit. When I laid down, I started feeling even worse. This was when my cold sweats started and I felt like someone had beat my whole body with a hammer. I began to shake uncontrollably while I was wrapped in my blanket. It felt like my throat was closing up and I began to cough as well. When I coughed, it felt as if there were razor blades in my throat and chest. I have a pretty high pain tolerance, so I tried to tough it out in my rack.

After a few more hours, I couldn't take it anymore. I peeled myself out of my rack and made my way to medical. They took a look at me, gave me some meds, and told me to get some rest. As I laid back down in my rack, I heard someone ask, "Master Chief Ramos, are you in here?" It was a sailor from medical. He asked me to please gather some toiletries and head back to medical, where I was to be quarantined for several days. I've never felt so sick in my life. I truly thought I might die in my bed. Makin Island's medical team took care of me over the next three days, and I finally started to feel better. Others weren't as lucky and had to stay for as long as ten days. I remember glancing around and thinking we all looked like we were on our deathbeds. It was kind of creepy.

It was clear we had an outbreak, even though we weren't able to test for COVID yet. Soon after, the Makin Island team implemented safety measures to help mitigate the spread of COVID. That was a tough task with such tight quarters, but we made it work. I had some lingering effects from the virus, including difficulty taking deep breaths for at least five months following my bout with the virus.

Shortly after that, we returned home and discovered COVID was in full force. It hit the world and our Navy hard in so many ways. Before we knew it, it was time to go to sea again. There were more than a handful of Makin Island sailors who were COVID positive or were close contacts that prevented them from going to sea with us. It even affected the Makin Island's Command Master Chief, the top master chief on the ship who works alongside the Commanding and Executive Officer. He had to stay behind and quarantine. I was hand-selected to fill in for him at sea as acting Command Master Chief. That was one of the most difficult duties of my career. There were so many unknowns and unanswered questions. Sailors were not only concerned for their well-being at sea in such close quarters, but more so for their loved ones at home while we were gone. And all of this was on top of having to take care of the mission. That was the longest at sea period ever! But the Makin Island leaders and crew rose to the challenge and made the mission happen.

A seven month deployment was now upon us. We knew it would be a huge challenge with COVID full steam ahead. Prior to deployment, we were quarantined for 3 weeks in a local hotel. I was appointed as the Senior Enlisted Leader there for over 500 sailors and Marines. I was responsible for ensuring their well-being for those 3 weeks. You can only imagine how many phone calls I received a day while everyone quarantined. No one could leave their quarters. We had to eat in our rooms, with no visitors, deliveries, or alcohol allowed. I could sit and tell you all the headaches from dealing with that, but we'd be here forever. After 21 unending days, we were escorted straight to the ship for a long 7 month COVID combat deployment. One of the most difficult in my career.

There were many things in place to help with the spread of COVID. We weren't able to work out, get haircuts, meetings were kept to a minimum, masks were always on, and the worst part was no port visits. Well, we still stopped in port, but we couldn't go out in town. So new sailors coming out of boot camp didn't get the opportunity to see the world on their first cruise. Stress levels across the board were at an all-time high. There were plenty of verbal and physical fights out of frustration. The leadership on board did the best we could to make life as comfortable as possible. All while keeping the mission first on a combat deployment. I was frustrated and stressed just like everyone else. The whole deployment just didn't feel right. But soon it was behind us and my four year tour on Makin Island was just about over.

You start to keep track of all the little things you miss while you're deployed. A good WiFi connection, being able to shower without shower shoes on, taking a bath in a real tub, not having to wait on a sink to wash your face or brush your teeth. You miss stand alone toilets and showers when your only option is a stall for both. Peeing alone is a luxury. Your time isn't your own. You can't eat what you want, when you want, and you can't cook. You don't decide when you sleep, and forget napping. There's no watching TV with a feel good drink or a cold beer on the couch. You can't listen to music as loud as you like. You don't get to lounge on your bed, and then add worrying about falling off the bed if you roll over more than once. You can't pick up the phone and call or text whoever you like whenever you want. There is no privacy. You can't hop in the car and just go for a drive. But the top thing from one person to the next is always the same. You miss your family like crazy. I'm always acutely aware of how much I miss my two children, friends, and family on every deployment. It never gets easier.

I made it to the highest enlisted rank in the United States Navy and in the military. I have so many people to thank for helping me make master chief, or master jefe. I can never repay their assistance, but only pay my blessing forward. I'm living proof that no matter where you're from or what you were doing before, your success can be born out of that struggle. The hardships can fuel you. Even if you start out in the ghetto, you can still succeed in life, in the military, and in any other profession. It takes an insane amount of work, and it often requires someone taking a chance on you. But you have to take that first step. And once you start walking towards your goals, find a mentor, advocate for yourself, and just keep pushing.

CHAPTER 26

I'm often asked how I've been successful in the Navy. The truth is, there's no secret to it. There's no blueprint, password, or book on how to make it to the top. At least not that I've seen. But that's not to say I didn't employ specific strategies to help me advance. I've tried to compile the advice I most often give to my sailors below. Some suggestions are military-specific, but most of it can be applied to any field. Challenge yourself to incorporate some of these tips, and watch as they work their magic.

I turned everything I learned in the hood into a positive and used it to my advantage in the military. Just like I always spent time getting my Nike Cortez bright white, and steamed those creases into my Ben Davis shirts, I put even more effort into my appearance in the Navy. I always had a sharp, clean, squared away uniform and my boots were shiny as hell. Presentation is everything. It represents pride in everything you do and respect for those that have served before us. And we all know that even though it isn't right, everyone judges a book by it's cover. If your uniform looks like shit and you look like shit, then they'll think you're worth shit. Perception is reality. That's half the battle to succeed when you first join the Navy. If you can keep your appearance tight, you're paving the way for your success.

I did what I was told and never complained. I followed orders and never gave push back unless it was absolutely necessary. For example, if the order was unsafe, didn't make sense, or I had a better solution, then I spoke up. More times than not, my supervisors took it onboard. Maintain a positive attitude, because it will yield positive results. If a door closes on you, continue to respectfully knock until it finally opens. Otherwise, I kept my mouth shut, listened, and did every job to the best of my ability. Never make excuses, just produce results. No half-assed products here. I relate that to cleaning up in the bathroom. Who only wipes half of their ass?

Be on time. Being punctual in the Navy paints the picture that you can be counted on to be present, and are always ready to get the job done. If you're 15 minutes early to your appointed place of duty, you're late. This kind of time management will also cover your ass in the event of an unexpected problem or delay. And it greatly reduces your stress level day-to-day when you aren't always behind schedule. In my 23 years of service, I can count on one hand how many times I've been late. Showing up ready to take care of business speaks volumes.

Become a subject matter expert. I vowed to become a master of my craft and to know my job inside and out. I added every qualification I possibly could and kept my head in the books by studying technical manuals, standard operating procedures, maintenance requirement cards, and picked the brains of senior personnel who were already experts. Think of it like this; when I joined the Navy, I was issued an imaginary tool bag. And it started out empty. Through studying, mentorship, and experience gained through hard work, I've slowly added tools. Leadership tools, maintenance tools, life tools, and many more that I can pull out at any time. I use them to assist myself and others as soon as we're met with a problem. Start filling your own toolbag, and it will come in handy when you need it most.

Study. Part of advancing to the next higher pay grade in the Navy means passing advancement exams filled with questions about job-specific and general military knowledge. I blew those exams out of the water, not because I'm smart or educated. We've discussed that I'm far from that. But I always had a solid study plan, was a master of my craft, and knew my job well. My plan was simple, but find what works for you and stick to it. My schedule may not fit into your life. I gathered all study material months before the exam, and studied an hour a day, five days a week. I took the weekends off as a reward. For that hour, I accepted no calls or messages, because it was my time and no one else's. I was consistent, and when the thought crossed my mind that studying was boring or I wished I were doing something else, I reminded myself what was at stake. I refocused on my motivation. If I didn't advance, I was leaving money on the table, delaying my career and leadership opportunities, and preventing myself from giving my kids everything I didn't have growing up.

Set both short and long-term goals. I always had goals in mind and kept my eye on the prize. I kept a list of both personal and professional short and long-term goals that my mentors helped me establish and execute. I set reasonable deadlines for myself and then made a plan to reach them. I held myself accountable. When I achieved them, I treated myself to things I enjoyed, like a trip to my favorite steak house, a vacation, and even materialistic things. And when I didn't stay on plan, I took away things I liked to motivate myself to work harder. I've learned that you have to apply yourself to achieve your goals. No one is going to hand them to you. You need to go out and get it! Don't waste time wishing, set manageable goals, execute each step along the way, and accomplish your dreams.

Treat everyone with dignity and respect. But I strongly believe that respect is earned, and one way to earn it is through honesty. I keep it real 100 and never sugarcoat anything. My honesty with my shipmates goes a long way to establishing trust. I share my life experiences so they can see I've struggled too, and provide them with the tools that helped me succeed. I'll be a hard ass when I need to be, or more sensitive depending on what the situation calls for. My aim is to treat everyone fairly and never show favoritism. When one of us wins, we all win. I have always been a huge advocate of equal opportunity regardless of race, gender, religion, sexuality, and color of skin in the military. If you can get the job done, then I'm your number one fan and you have my full support. Your performance matters to me, not what you look like or where you've come from. All this led to sailors who wanted to work for me and with me. They were willing to work hard to make me proud. A lot of time I would hear that part of their motivation was they didn't want to disappoint me.

Use adversity as fuel. The haters and terrible leaders have actually helped me be successful. And let me tell you, there have been a lot of them from both my time in the streets and in the Navy. These are people who wanted to see me fail or doubted that I would ever amount to anything. I always kept a positive chip on my shoulder from these people, but never fell into the trap of letting them control how I feel. I want to thank them for being a driving force for me to succeed. You can use adversity to your advantage. You do it quietly by succeeding in life and in your career. Through things like running a marathon, advancing to the highest position in your field, owning a house or a nice car, and maybe even writing a book one day. So, shoutout to all the haters and terrible leaders out there. We love you, forgive you, and thank you for motivating us to prove you wrong. The world would be a better place without the unnecessary adversity, but until then fuel your fire with their negativity.

Find a work life balance that suits you. No one should live to work; you should work to live. Otherwise, you'll burn yourself out. I've learned to use my time wisely at sea and at home. I prioritized what matters and managed my time well so I could do things I enjoyed to relieve work stress. Working out, going for a drive, treating myself to a nice meal, and visiting family and friends helped recharge my mind. Take that time for self-care, because you can't pour from an empty cup. Sometimes we get so invested in work that we neglect our home life. The next thing you know, you have built up pressure like steam in a pipe. Find ways to open up those relief valves or you'll burst and shut down. Once I left the office, I didn't think about work until I parked my car and headed in the next day, unless something urgent came up. Everyone needs time to breathe and decompress outside of work. Also, to my Navy shipmates, please take your shore duty. Everyone needs time to recharge. Back-to-back-to-back ships wear you down physically and mentally. Take care of yourself and your relationships through shore duty.

Most importantly, find a mentor. Mentors have been a huge part of my success. I've been fortunate to have several in my career that have paved the way and laid down the foundation for me to succeed. They will cheer on your wins, coach you after your losses, and keep you accountable as you chase your goals. Find someone that you want to emulate, that you want to be like one day, and pick their brain to find out how they got there. Keep in mind your imaginary tool bag and store all of the personal and professional life tools they hand you. Put them to use when the time comes, and also pass them down to your mentees. Special thanks to my mentors in the Navy. You set me up for success, and I consider you true friends – Master Chief (Retired) Drew Chinloy, Chief (Retired) Balt Hernandez, Master Chief (Retired) Rich Berger, Command Master Chief Rob Everson, Master Chief (Retired) Kemmy Frazier, Master Chief Mark Sowell. I also want to give a shout to those who have been true friends and have made a positive impact on my career and life, Chief (Retired) Rafa Orozco, Senior Chief Gus Ferreo, Senior Chief Sean Valis, Chief (Retired) June Angeles, and my mentee Chief Warrant Officer Gustavo Carrillo. This is far from an exhaustive list and I apologize if I didn't mention you, you know who you are!

I have seized almost every opportunity the Navy has given me. The life I've been able to create for my family and my kids is one I dreamed of but was scared was out of my reach. It has changed me for the better. I have seen places in the world that I could never have imagined visiting. I've been to Thailand, Dubai, Australia, Japan, China, India, Bahrain, Hong Kong, Guam, Hawaii, Canada, Singapore, Korea, Oman, Tasmania, and Malaysia to name a few. I've met some pretty amazing humans from all walks of life and I've had some experiences that I will hold on to and cherish forever. I served more than half of my life and I feel accomplished, and more importantly, I believe I've positively impacted every sailor I have encountered.

There is zero doubt in my mind that if the Navy had not given me a chance, I would be in jail for the rest of my life or six feet under right now. I took the lifeline and ran with it. And it taught me that anything is possible and achievable in this world if you're willing to work hard enough. But I also learned that we have to be willing to open doors for people behind us. My success was only possible because my mom made me realize I needed to finish school. I finished school because Miss "G" believed in me and motivated me. The Navy was only accessible because the CO at MEPS granted me a waiver. I found incredible mentor after mentor who coached me into a real leader and a better version of myself. Once you walk through a door that was previously closed to you, open it for someone else. I wouldn't be here without those generous people.

I hope that kids who've had a rough start like me can see that the world may have more to offer than we were led to believe. But you may not be as lucky as me. I have more lives than a cat and have escaped being imprisoned and shot by the grace of God. It's nothing I'm proud of. Just speaking facts. There's two things that are an almost certainty when you join a street gang. Jail time or death. There's more to life than running the streets in the hood trying to earn your stripes. Yes, getting out of the hood is easier said than done. But it's not impossible. Si se puede! Yes, you can! You have to find a way. Seize opportunities and make the right choices early before it's too late. Opportunities won't just fall in your lap, you have to go and get them. Stay in school. School was one of the few key reasons I was able to join the military and change my life.

The only thing I regret about serving in the Navy is all the lost time with my kids as they were growing up. I beat myself up about that. I can never get that time back. I can't erase the deployments, the missed birthdays and holidays, and being absent from special moments. Each experience compounds the previous. I'll never truly get past missing my son being born. My daughter has had struggles and difficulties in her life and I haven't been there to support or guide her, and that has destroyed me internally. I feel like I owe them both a huge debt.

But then I ground myself and understand that I didn't have control over that. I didn't choose to leave. I was away serving our great country, so we can continue to enjoy our liberties and freedoms and keep our enemies at bay. These two young blessings are my world and are my primary motivation in life. I had to sacrifice because I wanted them to have everything I didn't have and then some. I know I can't make up for lost time, but as my Navy career winds to a close, I can tell you that I'm looking forward to paying that debt. I'm thrilled that with retirement will come the freedom to be available to my children. I can only hope they will understand that dad was gone to serve this great country we live in. By no means have I been a perfect father, but I've always had their best interest at heart and would give anything to make them happy.

When I retire from the Navy, my goal is to work with at-risk youth in inner city schools and neighborhood programs. That would be a dream come true. I'd love to open some doors for kids like me in the next generation. I had the opportunity to speak in my uniform to young people in San Diego juvenile hall and at a school in Salinas, California. It's time to go and start the next volume of my story.